Jan Dressler's Guide to Beautiful Stenciling

Jan Dressler's Guide to Beautiful Stenciling

Sterling Publishing Co., Inc. New York
A Sterling/Chapelle Book

Chapelle, Ltd.:
Jo Packham
Sara Toliver
Cindy Stoeckl

Editor: Jennifer Luman
Copy Editor: Marilyn Goff
Layout: Jan Dressler
Staff: Kelly Ashkettle, Areta Bingham, Donna Chambers, Emily Frandsen, Karla Haberstich,Lana Hall, Mackenzie Johnson, Susan Jorgensen, Melissa Maynard, Barbara Milburn, Lecia Monsen, Suzy Skadburg, Kim Taylor, Linda Venditti, Desirée Wybrow

If you have any questions or comments, please contact:
Chapelle, Ltd., Inc., P.O. Box 9252,
Ogden, UT 84409
(801) 621-2777 • (801) 621-2788 Fax
e-mail: chapelle@chapelleltd.com
web site: www.chapelleltd.com

Library of Congress Cataloging-in-Publication Data

Dressler, Jan.
  Jan Dressler's guide to beautiful stenciling / Jan Dressler.
     p. cm.
  Includes index.
  ISBN 1-4027-1033-X
  1. Stencil work. I. Title: Guide to beautiful stenciling. II. Title.
TT270 .D74 2004
745.7'3--dc22
                                    2003023245
10 9 8 7 6 5 4 3 2 1
Published by Sterling Publishing Co., Inc.
387 Park Avenue South, New York, NY 10016
©2004 by Jan Dressler
Distributed in Canada by Sterling Publishing
c/o Canadian Manda Group, One Atlantic Avenue, Suite 105
Toronto, Ontario, Canada M6K 3E7
Distributed in Great Britain by Chrysalis Books
64 Brewery Road, London N7 9NT, England
Distributed in Australia by Capricorn Link (Australia) Pty. Ltd.
P. O. Box 704, Windsor, NSW 2756, Australia
Printed and Bound in China
All Rights Reserved

Sterling ISBN 1-4027-1033-X

To Pablo, who introduced me to the Diva within.You are the love of my life.

To Mom and Dad who always encouraged me, I love you.

To Aaron and Anna, my greatest works of art.

To all my friends and fellow stencil divas: hold your heads high, and never let the tiara tumble.

Introduction

I have a confession. I have not always been a Stencil Diva. I have not always known what I wanted to do. I have been afraid of the unknown, afraid of failure, afraid of doing something wrong, and very concerned about what people would think. I started out like so many women who, for unknown reasons, lack confidence in their ability to go it alone, to make it on their own strengths.

What changed my life? Stencils. I know, it sounds really weird; but it is the truth. I saw my first stencil and thought "what a neat idea." Even though I didn't feel that I could draw very well, I sat down and tried. I made my first stencil, applied paint through it, and I was transformed. I had found the tool that could beautifully express the creative spirit that has always been inside struggling to be free. And it happened just like that. One moment; one decision to try something new; I jumped off the edge and grew my wings on the way down.

It wasn't easy; there were times when I felt the fear of the unknown. But 15 years later, I am stronger and wiser—finally at peace with who I am and the road I have taken. I understand so much more about the importance of creativity, stepping out on my own and loving it. I am truly happy. This is what I have to share with you.

This book is for those of you who want to try something new, without fear. It is for anyone who was ever afraid of taking a class because they might look stupid! For anyone who ever wanted to color outside the lines, but did not for fear of ridicule! Yes, it is for you!

So often we are our own worst critics. "Oh, I've stenciled, but it sure didn't look like that"; "I'm not an artist"; "I don't have a creative bone in my body"; "I can't even finger-paint"; I have heard all of these things from people who have seen me giving demonstrations. I can't help smiling when I hear them! I turn and hand them the stencil brush and walk them through their first attempt. As the stencil is removed, a new being emerges from behind the mask of doubt and fear. A diva has peeked her head around the side of the mask, she's dusting herself off, straightening her hair, standing up tall and saying, "What took me so long?" They leave with a new sense of self. And it doesn't end there. They sign up for classes; they are stenciling their homes; then they are stenciling their friends homes; then the friend comes to take classes. They're paying it forward.

This book has been waiting for you. Now you hold it in your hand, and if you keep turning the pages, you will learn things that will change how you see yourself. This book will reduce your fear of not knowing how to get started, because I will tell you absolutely everything you need to know. It will reduce your fear of doing something wrong, because I have already done everything there was to do wrong, and I lived to tell the tale. If you already know how to stencil, you will learn a new technique. If you know my technique, you will learn some tricks that will make your stenciling go much faster. I hope that you will find some magic within these pages, something that will make you smile, and give you the confidence to try something new. There is nothing to fear. The journey has begun.

Table of Contents

Stencil Stuff

$\mathbf{A}$ contemporary stencil is nothing more than a template cut from a sheet of thin plastic. The thickness of the plastic varies, and the thinner the plastic, the easier the stencil is to work with. The majority of good quality stencils are laser-cut from 5-mil Mylar®. The Mylar is translucent, allowing you to see through it; and it is flexible, allowing it to adapt to different surfaces. The openings on the stencil represent the image that will be transferred onto a work surface during the stenciling process.

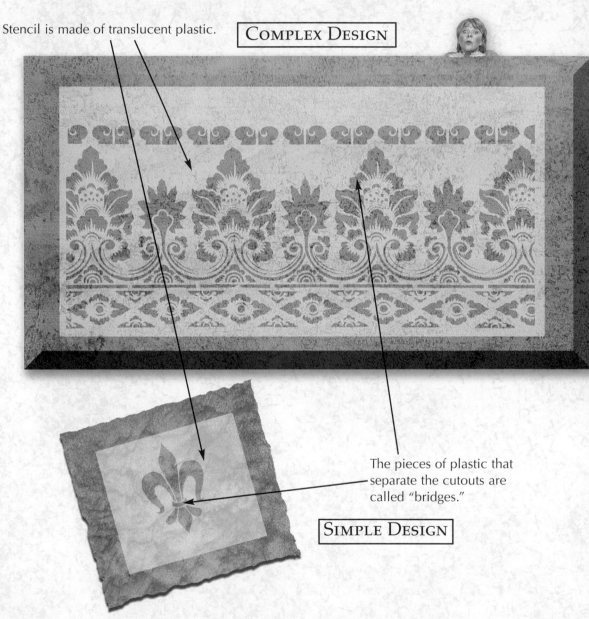

Stencil is made of translucent plastic.

COMPLEX DESIGN

The pieces of plastic that separate the cutouts are called "bridges."

SIMPLE DESIGN

The image can be simple or complex, and consist of one sheet of plastic or many. A single-sheet design can be a very basic shape, or a combination of complex shapes. The cutouts are separated from each other, leaving narrow bands of the plastic stencil called "bridges." A stencil designed in this way is called a "bridged" stencil. The result is reminiscent of block prints and can be very effective in allover wallpaper patterns and graphic borders.

A multiple-sheet design is one that is more complex in structure. The multiple sheets are called overlays and each one contains different parts of the total design. The images can have bridges or be bridgeless. Bridgeless designs are often referred to as "theorem-cut" designs and are more realistic, without having the gaps between the cutouts. This type of design has more flexibility in its use of color and application technique.

MULTIPLE OVERLAY STENCILS

COMPLETED IMAGE

The overlays are numbered in order of application. First you position overlay 1, stencil it, remove it; position overlay 2, stencil it, re-move it; and so on, until all are done and you have a complete print!

When multilayered stencils first came on the market, the overlays were commonly used to separate single colors. The first overlay may have been for green leaves, the second for pink flowers. But with the advent of more sophisticated designs came the need to stray from this restrictive practice. Why couldn't you use more than one color per overlay? Why not use more than one color per opening? It was a quantum leap forward, and brought stenciling into the modern design arena.

Y̶ou will find a vast array of stencils on the market. You can find them at craft stores, by mail order, on the Internet, and at specialty stencil stores. Typically, craft stores sell simple, single overlay designs that are die-cut or router-cut. Because of the manufacturing process, these designs are not very detailed. They are good for small simple projects and kid's crafts. Be aware of the thickness of the plastic and the stiffness of the stencil. Too much of either quality will negatively affect your project.

Simple die-cut stencils are good for craft projects, but can be too stiff and too thick.

Laser cut designs are usually more detailed and sophisticated. Five-mil Mylar is good for any application, it hugs the surface and bends around corners. These stencils can be more pricey.

If you are looking for detail and sophistication, you will be happier with a laser-cut stencil. The majority of laser-cut stencils are marketed by the many independent companies founded by artists who discovered the beauty of stenciling and applied their own unique talents to the art form. These companies are usually small businesses who depend upon advertising for their customer base. A very good way to find them is on the Internet, advertising in the back of the home decorating magazines, or at specialty stencil stores which carry a good selection of designer stencil lines.

There is a wide variety of designs to choose from, but be aware that all stencil companies are not made equally. The design may be fabulous, but there may not be instructions for use. So be certain to do your homework first.

Diva's Checklist

Call the company whose product you are using and ask questions. Much can be learned by the way your questions are fielded.

- Ask for the measurements of the stencils that interest you to be certain that the design will fit in the space you have envisioned for it.

- Ask about the instructions. Are they detailed and specifically written for the design that you've chosen or are they generic, leaving you on your own for color selection and application? Some stencils do not have good instructions and if you are not an experienced stenciler, you may not have the expertise to use them. It is best to know that up front.

- Does the company offer customer support? Will you be able to call for help if you need it? Will there be someone who is willing to help you?

- As with anything that you buy sight unseen, you may need to return the item. Check out the return policy before you buy. Items are usually subject to a restocking charge and may also have other requirements, such as not being opened. So, when you receive the product, hold it up to your space before you open it. See if it is going to fit. If not, follow the return policy to the letter.

  You should always call before you return the product. You may need to get an authorization number and be certain to insure the package for the value of the item. You will be responsible for the condition of the stencil until it gets back to the manufacturer, so protect yourself, and spend a few cents to insure the package. Remember that these companies are usually very small and their products are their livelihood. If the returned stencil arrives damaged, they cannot resell it and they won't refund your money.

- Likewise, if your stencil order from the company arrives in less than perfect condition, call and let them know. A reliable company will have insured the package and will replace the damaged item. They will usually get a replacement out to you right away, but just be certain of all that when you place your order.

- Be aware of the length of time you will have to wait for your product. Some companies operate on a vapor market, meaning that they don't actually have the item in stock; they need to have it manufactured and it could take up to six weeks for some companies to ship your order.

Whom you get your stencil and are confident that it is exactly what you want, it's a really good idea to remove the stencil from the package and check it out before you start pouring paint. A good quality design will come with detailed instructions which will tell you the size of the design, the length of the repeat (if it is a border design), how many overlays the design has, the colors of paint that will be used, the size and number of brushes you will need, and where to place each color of paint. Count the overlays and stack them in order to see that all the sheets are there.

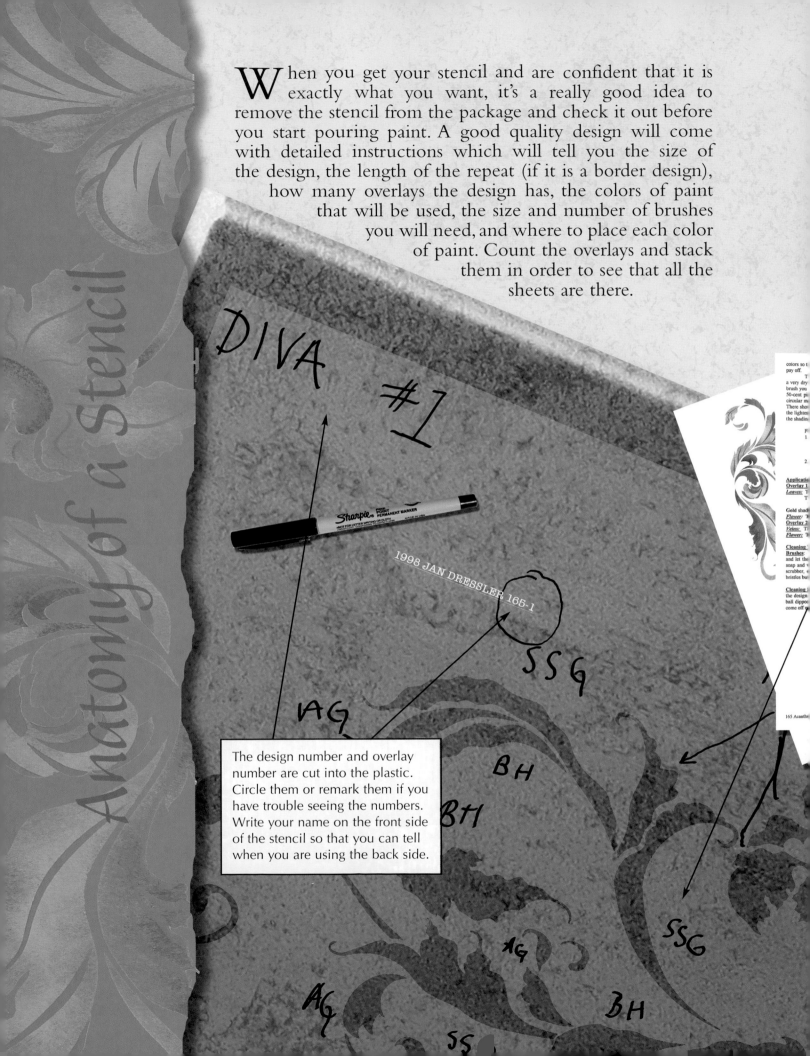

DIVA #1

1998 JAN DRESSLER 165-1

SSG

AG

BH

BH

AG

SSG

AG

BH

SS

The design number and overlay number are cut into the plastic. Circle them or remark them if you have trouble seeing the numbers. Write your name on the front side of the stencil so that you can tell when you are using the back side.

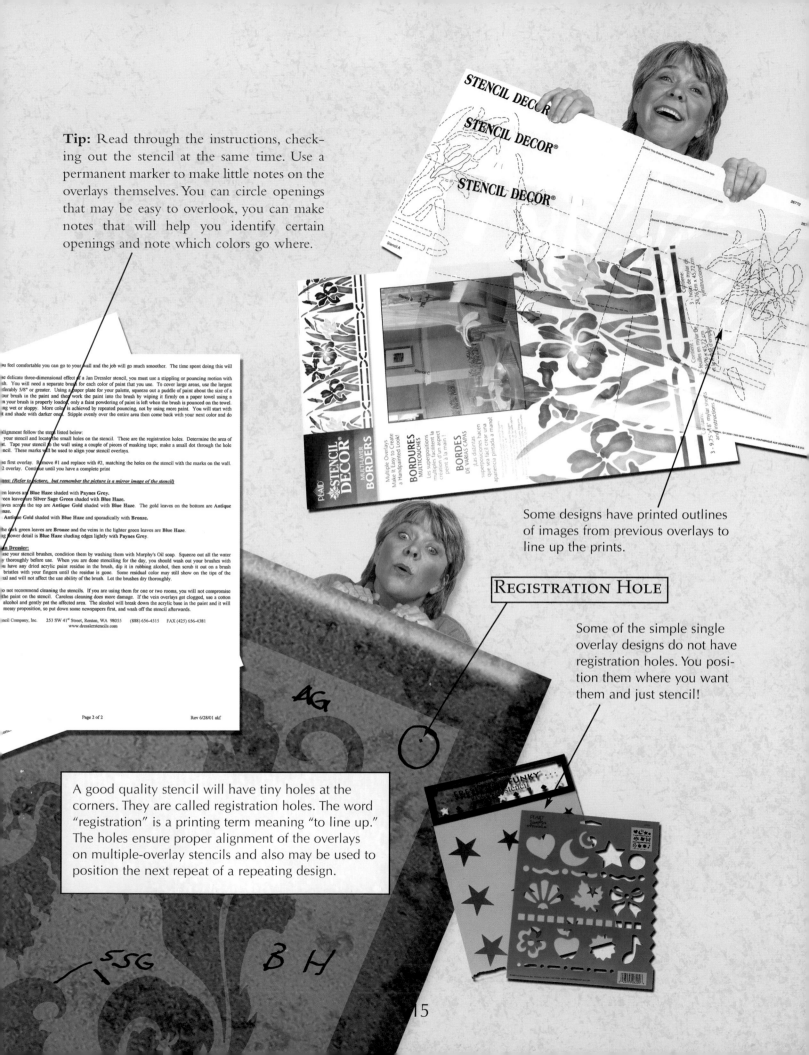

Tip: Read through the instructions, check-ing out the stencil at the same time. Use a permanent marker to make little notes on the overlays themselves. You can circle openings that may be easy to overlook, you can make notes that will help you identify certain openings and note which colors go where.

Some designs have printed outlines of images from previous overlays to line up the prints.

REGISTRATION HOLE

Some of the simple single overlay designs do not have registration holes. You position them where you want them and just stencil!

A good quality stencil will have tiny holes at the corners. They are called registration holes. The word "registration" is a printing term meaning "to line up." The holes ensure proper alignment of the overlays on multiple-overlay stencils and also may be used to position the next repeat of a repeating design.

There are many types of paint on the market, and what you use will depend upon your project. Paint manufacturers have developed specialty paints for every surface you can think of. New formulas are constantly being introduced and it is a real accomplishment to keep up with it. I have some recommendations for you though.

In my humble opinion, there is no product better than pre-mixed craft acrylics for stenciling on latex-painted walls and craft projects. The quick-drying characteristics of acrylic paint make the job go quickly and successfully. Colors can be layered almost immediately. The depths of hue, range of available colors, and ease of clean-up make acrylics my paint of choice.

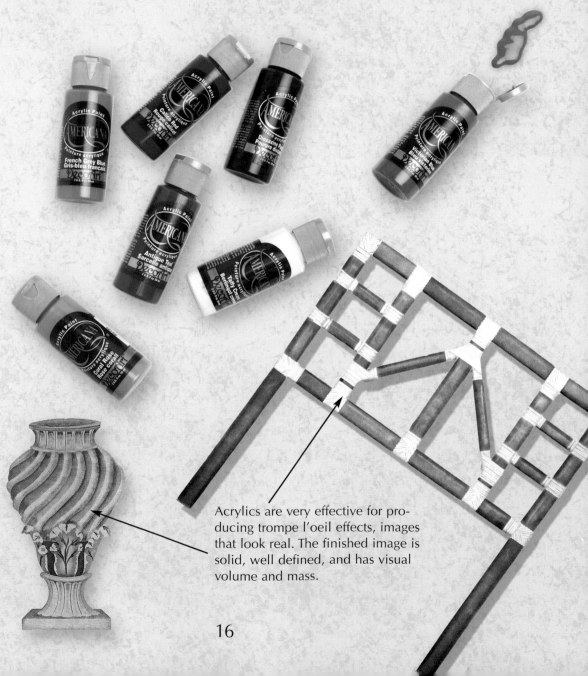

Acrylics are very effective for producing trompe l'oeil effects, images that look real. The finished image is solid, well defined, and has visual volume and mass.

16

Because they are a water-based paint, the emulsion may tend to separate in the bottle if it has stood undisturbed for a while. You will want to gently shake the paint bottles prior to use, to mix them up again. Place your thumb on the top of the bottle, just in case. You don't want the paint to splatter on your walls.

There are many mediums that can be added to acrylic paints that make them perfect for stenciling on other surfaces.

When paint conditioner is added to acrylic paint, it thins the paint without diluting the color. It's great for faux finishing and brush painting.

Some paints can be used on metal surfaces such as mailboxes, tinware, even those chrome shower doors.

Glass can also be stenciled using acrylic enamels.

Faux glazing liquid turns a bit of acrylic paint into a glaze for faux finishing.

Fabric medium mixed into acrylic paint allows you to match the colors that you use on the wall, but make the decorated fabric washable as well.

There are specially formulated paints for exterior stenciling, either on wood, plaster, cement, or terra-cotta.

There are special acrylics for waxy surfaces like candles.

17

Whe your surface is painted with an oil-based paint, you must also use an oil-based paint product for stenciling. Acrylics will not bond with the surface and will rub off. There are a couple of oil-based products that can be used successfully.

Paint Creams

These paints are oil-based paint in cream form, and look a bit like shoe polish. They can be used on latex paint as well, and produce a very translucent print. I use them in conjunction with acrylic paint, for creating drop shadows, delicately shading edges, and for defining shapes.

Author's Note: Throughout the text, when I refer to paint creams, I am using Decoart Easy Blend Pant Creams. I have found that this is the only kind that works for this process.

I use the paint creams for all my shadowing. The cast shadows within the arch of this trompe l'oeil doorway have been done with a black cream paint wiped over with mineral spirits. The result is very realistic!

Paint creams can help to delicately define edges on both light and dark colors. It does not affect the acrylic paint underneath.

Alkyd-oil Artist Colors

I use these artist oils on floors that will need to be sealed with a chemical topcoat. I use a cobalt drying agent to speed up the drying time of the oils. Be certain that you have lots of ventilation; a good ventilator mask is a must. Oil paints are very workable and you will need to constantly clean your stencil if you are using many colors and/or overlays.

Tip: Oil-based paints are best when used on simple single-overlay designs that don't require a lot of colors. If you use more than one color, you will want to clean off the stencil after each print. The reason for this extra cleaning is that the oil-based paint remains workable and your brush will pick up any paint residue remaining on the edges of the cutouts. Soon your colors will be all mixed together and become a muddy brown color.

The Stencil Diva's stenciling tool of choice is a good quality stencil brush. If you get good brushes, you are far more likely to achieve great results.

Brushes come in many sizes; my favorite size is a full 1"-diameter brush. It will give you good overall coverage and good edge effects as well. Smaller brushes can be used for detail work and small isolated areas of color, but your main openings on the stencil should be printed using the larger brush.

At first, you may be tempted to get small brushes because they are less expensive. But small brushes make the job go much more slowly. You need to reload the brush more often, and your finished print will have a dappled look. Believe me, if you spend a dollar more per brush for the larger size, it will be the best investment you ever made.

The handle should be stained and lightly varnished. Painted or glossy varnished handles will end up cracking and peeling, leaving your brush handle unprotected. The unprotected wood absorbs water and expands. When it dries out, the wood shrinks and will eventually result in the loss of the entire bristle head.

Brush Sizes
If your stencil doesn't come with instructions listing brush sizes, a good rule of thumb is to use brushes that are larger then the openings you will be stenciling. Doing so will give you a better quality print.

Chip Brushes
Inexpensive white-bristle flat brushes are great for base-coating or adding background effects in murals.

A quality brush will last for years, and it is important to get an ample supply of them. You don't pay any more for a good brush than for a bad brush, so price won't be an indicator. You need to know what to look for.

The bristles themselves should feel silky to the touch and be flexible yet resilient. Run your thumb across the end of the bristles, they should spring back into place. If the bristles are too stiff, you will have to work too hard to get the paint out. If they are too soft, they will splay or separate in the center.

The ends of the bristles should be "flagged," resembling split ends on your hair. If the ends of each bristle are the same thickness from base to tip, it will be too hard to get paint out of the brush, and the brush will splay.

Stainless steel ferrule that doesn't dent under pressure from your fingers. Avoid aluminum ferrules, they are weak and the metal turns your fingers black, which can rub off onto your project. If the ferrule is dented, the brush will not produce an even print. The bristles within the dented area are more compacted and will make a darker spot.

Place the bristle end of the brush in the palm of your hand and make the brush do the hula. The end of the bristles should remain in place and not move in your hand, yet the base of the ferrule should be dancing away.

How Many Brushes Will You Need?

- In my honest and totally unbiased opinion, you can never have too many brushes.

- To complete a project, you need one brush for each color of paint that you are using. You cannot mix paint colors on one brush.

- The brushes have to remain dry throughout the stenciling project, so you can't wash one out and use it for another color. The water would run down the bristles and dilute the paint and it would run right under the stencil.

- So start out with at least a dozen brushes. You can save your family hours of shopping simply by having them get you stencil brushes for every occasion.

When you have a large area to cover and want to have a uniform coat of paint, there is nothing like a high-density sponge roller to speed up the job. There are a few varieties out there in the marketplace, so shop carefully.

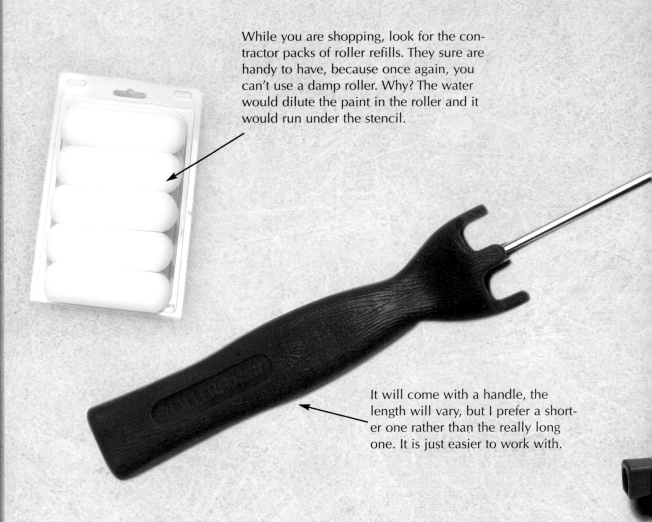

While you are shopping, look for the contractor packs of roller refills. They sure are handy to have, because once again, you can't use a damp roller. Why? The water would dilute the paint in the roller and it would run under the stencil.

It will come with a handle, the length will vary, but I prefer a shorter one rather than the really long one. It is just easier to work with.

Tip: It is a good idea to start with two setups. That way if you are working on a project that has two colors of paint to be applied, one over the other, you won't have to change the roller between applications.

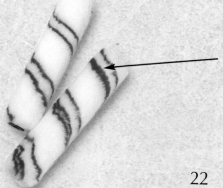

There are also fuzzy type rollers that are skinnier than the sponge type. They look kind of like the fur on your favorite teddy bear. These are commonly called cigar rollers. They work in a pinch; but they don't hold as much paint and, therefore, it takes longer to achieve an even coat.

The sponge part should be very dense, with a surface that does not have any holes. You don't want a really absorbent roller because it holds too much paint that can run under the stencil. The common length of the sponge refill is either 4" or 6".

Sponges

Good quality sea sponges are handy to have for adding texture to stone images and for doing simple faux finishes. Larger sponges are best for covering big areas, smaller ones for detail sponging. Store them dry, and be certain to soak them well prior to each use to keep the center of the sponge from breaking apart.

Zip-top plastic bags are handy too. You can slip one over the "painty" roller and seal it around the metal handle. This will keep them from drying out between applications. You can also save the rollers in the bags. Just slip the bag over the roller, pull it off the handle and seal the top. It will remain fresh for a long time. When you need to use it again, put the metal prong into the bag and slip on the roller. Your hands won't get all painty and your nails will stay nice.

Paint Tray

You will need a plastic paint tray that is made to fit the small rollers. Get a couple of these as well. If you can't find the little ones, then get a regular paint tray and some plastic pan liners. This will allow you to keep your colors of paint separate, and just trade liners when you are ready to switch colors.

W̲hether you are a beginning stenciler or a seasoned veteran, I have a tried-and-true list of supplies that will make each project go smoothly. You can keep them all in a toolbox so that you will never have to go hunting them down. There are only a few simple tools that you need to have in your toolbox.

Adhesives

In order to position your stencil on the wall or project surface, you will need some tape. I prefer blue painter's tape. It is very gentle to the painted surface and doesn't harm the wall surface or leave any residue on the wall. It's quite durable and can be used time and again. Best of all, it's easy to see.

You can use regular masking tape; but some are really sticky, so you will want to remove some of the tack by sticking it to your shirt and peeling it off. That way, it's much less likely to pull off any paint from the wall.

There are a few cases where you may find it necessary to use spray adhesives. Be aware that they are messy to use, and they can make your stencil extremely difficult to work with. The sprayed stencil either tends to stick to everything including itself and other overlays, or it doesn't stick at all!

Pencil

I use a mechanical pencil with .05 lead. It is always sharp and easy to identify as yours.

Carpenter's Level

You can get a 3' level at the hardware store that will come in very handy for establishing level lines either horizontally or vertically.

Palette

You need to have a flat surface to act as your art palette. I use a waxed paper plate or a sheet of waxed paper. If worse comes to worse, and you don't have those, you can use a ceramic dinner plate! Anything with a relatively nonabsorbent surface works just fine.

Tape Measure

A good quality tape measure is a must. Be certain the tape itself is 1" wide, has an auto retract, and a belt clip. I find that a 15' tape is the handiest. You can measure standard-size rooms easily, yet it's not too heavy to carry on your belt.

Blotter

This high-tech tool is a very important piece in the toolbox; in fact the success of your projects depend upon it: good old household paper towels! I prefer to use an absorbent type that feels like cloth.

Calculator

A small pocket calculator is handy. Use it religiously; even simple division should be checked because it is easier to check it than to figure out how you can adjust an image that has been miscalculated. Do the math twice, and paint once!

Carpenter's Belt

I wear a carpenter's belt or apron when I stencil. It has all the right pockets for brushes, a clip for your tape measure, a pencil pocket, and there's even room for a couple of bottles of paint. You are now all self-contained and have everything at your fingertips.

Blotter Folding Tip: I tear off two sheets, keeping them joined together. Fold them together, and then fold them both as one, one more time. This gives you a very good absorbent blotter that has a total of four separate blotting pages. As you use up one side, you can open it up like a book and use the following pages.

Odds & Ends

- Paint conditioner is a must have for many reasons. It keeps your brushes from drying out and is handy if you are using the foam rollers to apply a base coat on your stencils. It thins the paint without diluting the color. Add a couple of chip brushes. They're inexpensive and great for base-coating and blocking in color.

- You'll want a hair dryer for drying base coats and speeding up layering. One of the small folding ones is good; and a 12' extension cord will come in handy too.

- Push pins and some heavy-duty quilting thread are really handy for establishing guide lines. Just place the pins at the points of measurement, tie a loop in the end of the thread, and run it to the other pin, wrapping it around the shank.

- A heavy steel washer is good to use as a plumb bob. Tie it to a piece of thread and wrap the other end around a push pin. The resulting line will be perfectly vertical.

- Cotton swabs and a small container of all-purpose cleaner are important items for damage control. If you make a mistake with acrylic paint, dip the swab in the cleaner and gently rub it on the goof. It will come right off.

- A can of odorless mineral spirits is handy for using with paint creams.

- You'll want a clear-plastic grid ruler for measuring accurately.

- Extra stencil brushes and some chip brushes are always good to have.

- Carry a small screwdriver for removing switch plates, cleaning your nails, etc. I like the ones that have the interchangeable bits. Put your name on it as well.

- A paint can opener and a stir stick are also very good to have in there. You never know when you may need them.

- Some disposable plastic bowls and craft sticks for mixing small amounts of paint. Put in some rubber gloves too.

- You may as well throw in a retractable craft knife and a pair of scissors.

- Add a piece of glass for cutting and repairing stencils with your craft knife.

- A pack of peanuts or a candybar. When you're running on empty, it's good to know you've got emergency supplies!

Ladder

A sturdy ladder is very important to have when you are relying on it to support you and your paint. One with nonslip feet is preferred so that you don't go crashing to the floor by accident.

I use an articulated ladder, one of those that is double-jointed and can assume all different positions. I find it especially useful because you can climb up both sides of it and can cover quite a bit of territory before you have to move it. It can be a sizeable investment though, so if you are just starting out you may want to wait until you get the stencil addiction before you spend the big bucks!

Portable Work Surface

If you are standing on a ladder to stencil high on the wall, you can save time and prevent accidents by using a portable work surface. Climbing up and down a ladder to reload your stencil brush can be very time consuming and dangerous.

I have a simple solution. Find a cardboard box about the size of the top step of your ladder. Fold in the flaps and turn it upside down. Fit it over the top step of your ladder and tape it to the legs of the ladder. The result is a nice flat surface like a tabletop. Now you can tape down your palette, and your paper towel for blotting your brush. You won't need to get down from the ladder until you need to move to the next repeat! This is a very useful item and once you find a good one, take good care of it. Mine has lasted for about six years!

Note: Be certain to tape the box securely to your ladder. You also want to tape the plate in place.

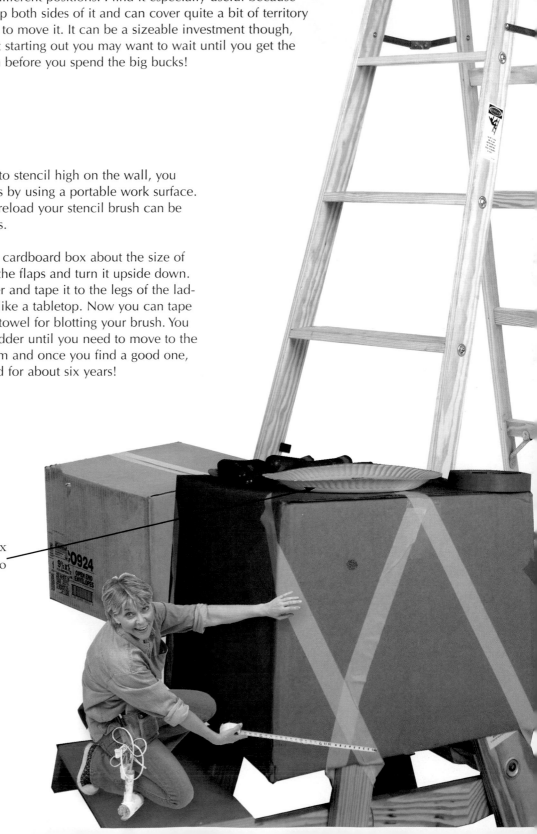

Diva's Stenciling Techniques

Diva's Color Theory

Now, I don't have any fancy degrees from accredited stencil colleges, but I have spent years at the school of hard knocks. When it comes to color theory, I have found that there are certain color combinations that make your heart feel good. The commonality of each combination is that they are balanced with a red tone, a blue tone, and a yellow tone. They are what I call full-spectrum combinations. Choose colors of similar intensity in order for the image to look comfortably balanced.

Reds Represented by:
Reds
Oranges
Pinks
Red-based browns
Plums
Peaches
Red violet
Red-based metallics
Any warm reddish color

Yellows Represented by:
Cool yellows
Golden yellows
Yellow greens
Bieges
Khaki
Yellow browns
Cream
Metallic gold
Any warm yellow color

Blues Represented by:
Blues
Blue violet
Dark value greens
Blue-based greens
Blue-toned grays
Blue purples
Lilacs
Metallic silver
Any cool blue or green color

Author's Note: In this book, I use and refer to Decoart Americana Acrylics and Easy Blend Stencil Paints. Use a paint color conversion chart to find comparable colors available from other manufacturers. You will find most of the color names to be pretty self-explanatory with the exception of Payne's Grey. This color is actually a very dark blue, so why they call it Grey is known only to the paint gods!

Shading colors helps to define the edges of colors that may otherwise fade out and lose their dimensional effect. Here are some combinations that work well for shading using acrylic as a base paint and paint creams for shading.

Base Colors:
(Acrylic)
Titanium White
Lemon Yellow, Yellow Light
Sand, Antique White, Golden Straw
Khaki Tan
True Blue, All dark blues
Metallics

Shading Colors:
(Paint Cream)
Baby Blue, Neutral Grey, Ebony Black, Charcoal Grey
Cadmium Yellow, Charcoal Grey, Ebony Black
Charcoal Grey
Charcoal Grey, Ebony Black
Ebony Black
Ebony Black

As a rule of thumb for dimensional shading with paint creams, you can use Ebony Black for rich deep colors like reds, browns, greens, greys, purples, and blues. Charcoal Grey or Neutral Grey work well for warm lighter colors like whites, bieges, peaches, yellows, and creams. Try them out. If the Charcoal Grey makes the image look dusty rather than rich, then opt for the Ebony Black.

When I am stenciling flowers and greenery, I like to add lots of colors. Here are some great combinations using acrylics for both base colors and shading colors:

Base Color:	Shading Color:
Peach tones	Cranberry Wine or Black Plum
Deep true red tones	Payne's Grey
Baby blue	Cranberry Wine, Payne's Grey
Yellows	Cranberry Wine, Black Plum
Pinks	Cranberry Wine
Greens	Payne's Grey, Soft Black, Black Green
Browns	Soft Black, Payne's Grey

Here are some tried-and-true combinations for specific images that work for me:

Leaves and Vines Without Flowers:
Taffy Cream: used in the center of the leaves to give them some life.
Forest Green: used around the edges of the leaves.
Russet: used for woody stems or added sporadically to the leaves.
Payne's Grey: used at the base and tips of the leaf for dimension.

Flowering Bushes and Vines:
Pink Flowers:
French Mauve with Cranberry Wine and a touch of Payne's Grey
Pink Chiffon with Raspberry and a touch of Black Plum

Peach Flowers:
Peach Sherbet with Cranberry Wine and Black Plum
Hi-Lite Flesh and Shading Flesh shaded with Charcoal Grey

Greenery:
Forest Green shaded with Payne's Grey
Light Avocado shaded with Payne's Grey, Soft Black or Ebony Black
Black Forest Green with Payne's Grey or Ebony Black

You will eventually make your own favorite combinations. Don't be afraid to experiment with color; remember, it is fun!

The Diva's Stencil Dogma

The Diva's Definitive Technique, also known as the DDT, uses multiple colors within each opening of the stencil. The lightest colors are applied first, creating the highlight and the darker colors are layered around the edges. This gives a very lovely glow to the image that can't be achieved in any other way. This technique is what will make your stenciling stand out. In fact, once you master this basic process, you can tackle any project and are well on the way to becoming a true "Stencil Diva." So pay attention, this will make a big difference in your final results. You'll be the envy of the neighborhood!

USE NO WATER!

The only water that you should have around you while stenciling is the bottled kind that has a pull-out spout. And the only place you will ever put that water is in your mouth. You will never, and I mean never, use it on your brush or in your paint. Stenciling is not like tole painting, water-color, or any other paint technique that you may have come across. Your brush will remain free of water until you are done for the day and need to clean up.

Honestly, the only real mistake that people make when they first try to stencil is they either dip their brush in water first, or they use too much paint on their brush. Both result in paint running under the edges of the stencil, making a sloppy mess.

1 Gather all your required colors of paint and prepare your paint palette. With each color that you will use, squirt out a 50-cent- piece-sized puddle of paint. Don't be cheap and use a quarter- sized instead, it is important to have enough paint to evenly cover the entire bristle end of the brush.

2 Prepare your blotter. Tear off the two towels, fold them together and then fold in half.

Now for THE ONLY THING YOU REALLY NEEDTO KNOW TO STENCIL SUCCESS-FULLY . . . THE THING THAT IF DONE WRONG WILL MAKE YOU FAIL IN YOUR QUEST TO ACHIEVE DIVA STATUS . . .

Loading Your Brush

1 Take one of your dry stencil brushes, of the proper size, (remember, the bigger the better,) and dip the brush into the puddle of paint. One firm dip is enough. Don't swish it through the paint, just one firm dip.

ha ha ha ha ha!!

2 Look at the brush to be certain that you have paint on the entire bristle surface.

Now I know what every one of you is saying, "What a terrible waste of paint!" Be that as it may, if you don't make the big swirlies, the paint won't be evenly distributed into the bristles, and you will end up with a blotchy-looking print, and a polka-dot effect.

Those of us who grew up in the '50s may remember polka dots, saddle shoes, and white anklets. Those things never have to return as far as I am concerned. So don't let them show up on your wall!

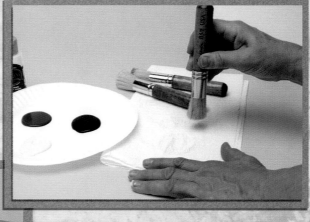

4 To test your efforts, tap the brush on a clean area of the paper towel. It should produce a light, even imprint of the bristle head. If you tap it on the back of your hand it will leave a powdery impression. Now your brush is properly loaded.

3 Move the loaded brush to your pad of paper towels. Then using firm pressure, work the paint into the bristles by making swirls about the size of a cookie on the paper towel.

Practicing the loading process is a good idea, and as long as your brush is loaded you may as well practice stenciling! Why waste all that paint and have to clean those brushes with nothing to show for it but a messy pad of paper towels.

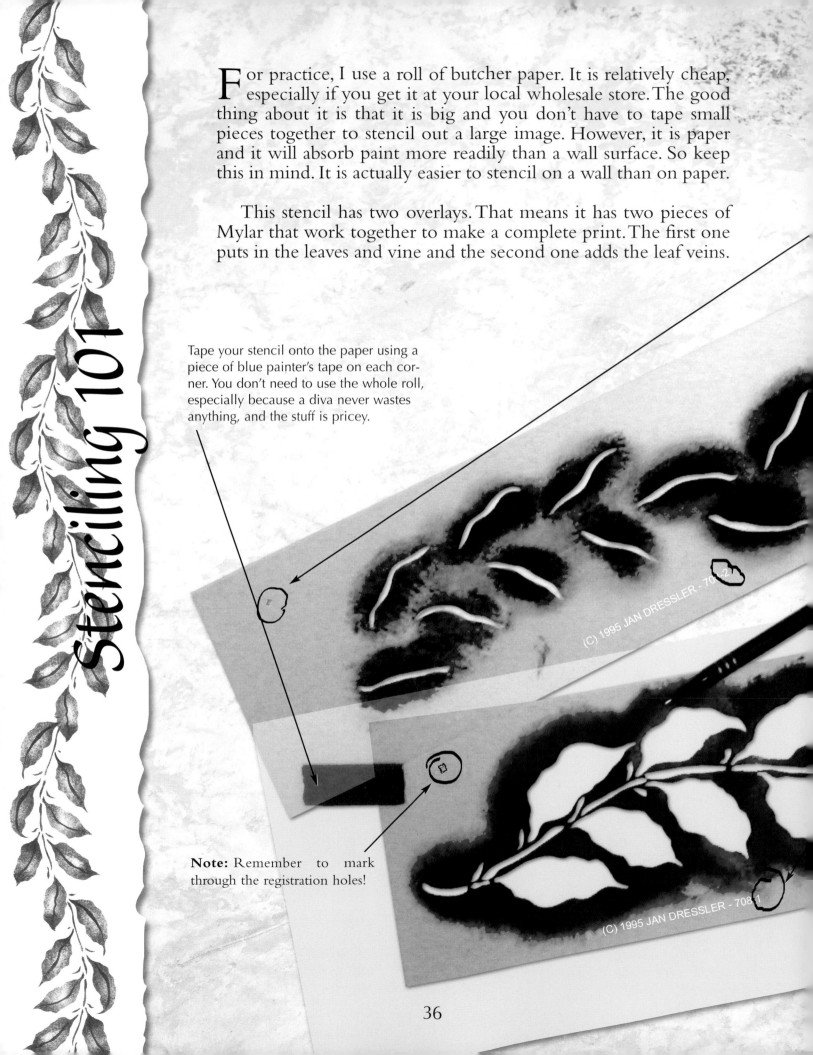

For practice, I use a roll of butcher paper. It is relatively cheap, especially if you get it at your local wholesale store. The good thing about it is that it is big and you don't have to tape small pieces together to stencil out a large image. However, it is paper and it will absorb paint more readily than a wall surface. So keep this in mind. It is actually easier to stencil on a wall than on paper.

This stencil has two overlays. That means it has two pieces of Mylar that work together to make a complete print. The first one puts in the leaves and vine and the second one adds the leaf veins.

Tape your stencil onto the paper using a piece of blue painter's tape on each corner. You don't need to use the whole roll, especially because a diva never wastes anything, and the stuff is pricey.

Note: Remember to mark through the registration holes!

36

Locate the registration holes at the corners of the design. Use your mechanical pencil to mark through the holes onto your paper. These marks will be used to line up the next overlay and act as placement marks for the next repeat of the design. When I am stenciling walls, I use the pencil to mark through onto the wall as well.

Note: You may hesitate to mark on your walls if you are the really picky type of person who notices every single detail in your surroundings. Now, don't get me wrong, that's not a bad thing . . . so in your case, use a couple more pieces of tape and slip them behind the plastic directly under the holes. Then you can mark on the tape and remove it when you have completed the entire print.

For the rest of us action junkies, you will really never be able to see them once the beoooty-full design is on the wall. In fact, I have a hard time finding them when they are right in front of me, so don't be too worried about it.

Locate overlay 1, it will be marked with the design number and the overlay number. Use a permanent marker to remark the overlay numbers so you can see them.

Put tape under the registration holes if you wish.

1 Always start with the lightest colors first; in this case, it is a pale yellow, Taffy Cream. I use this a lot in the centers of my leaves. It gives the leaf a nice sunny look. Load the brush according to the DDT. Apply the paint in a gentle but firm pouncing motion. Your brush will be coming directly down on the paper, through the stencil. There will be no chance of the paint running under the stencil, both because of the pouncing motion and because there is very little paint on the brush itself. Just do a few pounces of the yellow in the center of the leaf, you don't want to color the entire opening.

Note: Always start with your lightest colors first in whatever color range you are working with.

2 Load another clean dry brush with the next darker color, in this case Antique Teal, and apply the color around the edges of the openings. Center your brush more on the plastic than in the opening itself. This keeps the color out on the edges, gently blending the two colors. You can peek under the stencil at this point, being careful not to shift the Mylar. You will be able to determine whether or not you need to deepen the color. Everyone stencils differently, and your touch will determine how the final results will look. A light touch will make the design look ethereal. A firm touch will make the design more vibrant. Only you will know what effect you like best, so try all variations.

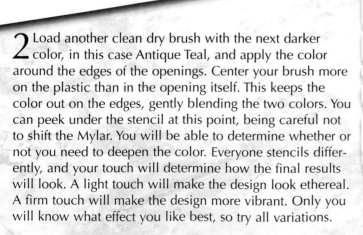

38

3 The last step on this overlay is to add sophistication with the dimensional color, Payne's Grey. You don't need much of it, all you want is a powdering of the tone. Focus the color at the base and tips of the leaves and at any points where the vines cross or end. If you can see the splotches of color, you have too much paint. To avoid this, use a larger brush and load it properly. It will diffuse the color. Remove this stencil and position overlay 2. Just match the holes in the Mylar with the marks from the first overlay. Tape it down like you did before.

4 Use the Payne's Grey brush and do the leaf veins, remove the stencil, and ta daaaa! You're done! Take some time to gaze upon the fruits of your labor. The result is totally amazing, and will elicit gasps of awe from the delighted onlookers.

Note: Now don't go and give up if you don't get the effect you want the first time; just keep practicing. As they say, a diva is not made in one day. If you have some splotchy-looking prints, don't worry. Just turn the page for some surefire, quick fix solutions!

Fixing Less Than Perfect Prints

There are some common mistakes that can be made. However, there are also ways to fix them. Most result from improper loading of the brush. Experience will teach you the most; there really is no reason that you should ever have a less than perfect print.

If the print is too pale, add more pounces of green around the edges.

If the print looks too splotchy, you have an unevenly loaded brush.

Reload and work the paint into the bristles again; then go very lightly and evenly over the area again, working for a consistent balance of color.

If the print is too dark, go back over it with the yellow, giv-ing it solid coverage. Dry it with a hair dryer and try again.

Tip: Remember it is better to start light as you can always add paint. It's harder to subtract paint.

Leave more pale yellow in the center. To do this, center your brush on the surrounding Mylar, rather than in the opening and just let a few of the bristles hang over into the opening.

Tip: When you are stenciling with acrylic paints, your brushes may tend to dry out, especially if you are working in a warm room, an air-conditioned room, or a space with a lot of air flow. They will get rather crunchy around the edges.

You can counteract this by dipping your brushes into a puddle of paint conditioner. Unload them very well, working the conditioner into the brush. This step will rejuve-nate the paint in the brush and keep it supple. If your brush dries out too much, you will need to replace it with a clean one. Wash out the dirty one and lay it to dry.

If you are using paint creams for your project, your technique will differ. This paint is very translucent and will produce a more delicate, faded print. If your entire project will be done with paint creams, be certain to test it out on a sample of your wall color first. Cream paints work really well on light neutral white-based colors, but can disappear on darker colored walls.

These paints are marketed as "No Mess" paints, but the name is very misleading. When you remove the lid, the paint has a tough layer of cured paint "skin" on the surface. You must first peel off the "skin," which is a messy process.

BE CAREFUL WITH THE SKINS THAT COME OFF.

Throw them away. I seal them into a zip-top plastic bag. Work over a drop cloth as you are using these paints because the little pieces of paint will grow into huge spots on the carpet, which are difficult if not impossible to remove. Some stencilers add a little water to the jar to keep the skin from forming, but just remember to have a container handy to dump out the water when you are ready to use the paint.

Tip: Try using a paper towel and twist firmly on the top of the paint pot. The skin will be dislodged and some will remain on the towel.

You will use a smaller stencil brush with paint creams than you would with acrylics. The size will depend upon the size of the stencil openings; but I find that a ¼"-diameter brush works well for large- and medium-sized openings if you need an even coverage. If you are outlining the openings, then use a brush that is ⅛" diameter or smaller.

Swirl the brush into the paint and unload it on a paper towel, lightly swirling the brush to get off any globs of paint.

You will then swirl the paint into the stencil cutouts, working from the outside inward. Be careful not to raise up the bridges between openings. If you need to use more than one color in the opening, use a paper towel to remove paint residue from the stencil first, then apply the second color with another brush.

Tip: If you are using a multiple-overlay stencil and cream paints, I recommend that you run only one overlay at a time. Complete your border using overlay 1; then after you are done, go back and use overlay 2. This will give the oil paint a little time to cure and it may not come off on the back of your successive overlays. You will still need to clean the stencil surface after every print though, to keep your colors pure.

Cleaning brushes is not fun, but it is necessary. It is much easier to clean your tools right after you have finished for the day than to leave them to get hard. Acrylic paint turns to cement if left to its own devices!

Two of the greatest inventions of all time are an all-purpose cleaner, and the brush scrubber. A brush scrubber is a little plastic pad with raised nubs, and you scrub your brush across it to remove the paint from inside the bristles. This is how I clean brushes.

Author's Note: To clean my brushes, I use Simple Green™ all-purpose cleaner. It is an environmentally safe cleaning liquid that breaks down acrylic paint like nothing else.

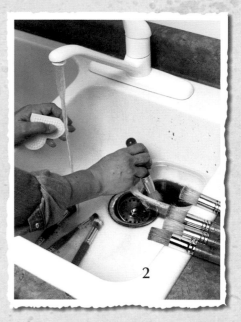

1 Don't soak your brushes. Too much water for too long can loosen up the glue that holds the bristles in the ferrule. Simply lay your brushes in the bottom of the sink and run really warm water over them. If the paint has hardened in the bristles, this will start to soften it.

2 Pour the undiluted all-purpose cleaner into a container. Take one brush, squeeze out the water in the bristles, and dip it into the cleaner.

Paint Creams

The paint creams clean up very well with liquid soap and water.

Oils

Oil paints need to be cleaned from the brush using odorless mineral spirits. Be certain to use enough to clean the brushes thoroughly.

Tips: To save time during cleanup, you can use a bit of paint conditioner to work into your brushes periodically during the day. That way, the paint won't have a chance to dry out and harden and it makes clean up a snap.

Use zip-top bags to keep your brushes moist.

Note: Brush cleaning is a wonderful behavior modifier. When my kids were small and they misbehaved, the consequences included cleaning stencil brushes. They quickly became model children!

3 Now, with the warm water running, work the brush into the scrubber, swirling it firmly across the nubs. Rinse out the brush, squeeze out the water, dip it again and scrub some more. Pretty soon the brush will be clean. Take care not to dilute the cleaner. It doesn't work nearly as well if it gets diluted.

4 Squeeze the excess water from the bristles and lay them on the edge of a counter with the bristles hanging over the edge. They will dry quicker that way. Placing them in a warm place helps. During the summer, you can lay them on your deck or windowsill and they will dry very quickly. I place them over the heat vent in my studio floor during the winter and they dry nicely.

Sponge Products

Sponges and rollers will be ruined if they are allowed to dry out. Keep your paint-covered sponges in a large bucket of water until you have time to rinse them out. Sponge rollers can be kept in zip-top bags, then rinsed out under cool water. Rinse until the water runs clear.

Cleaning Stencils

Cleaning your stencils is a time-consuming job. If you only plan on using the stencil for one job, you may not wish to spend the time cleaning it. I don't clean my stencils, preferring to have the color imprint on the plastic so that it is easier to tell where the colors go. However, if the openings in the stencil start clogging up, you will need to clean it. Just remember that careless cleaning does more damage than leaving the paint on.

Acrylic paint hardens as it dries, and the best way of gently removing the paint is to lay the stencil in the sink and cover it with very warm water. This will soften the paint and make it easy to gently massage the paint off of the plastic. Be careful not to raise up any of the delicate parts of the stencil.

Tip: If the paint is really hard to get off, take it out of the sink and place it into a plastic trashbag, spray it with full-strength cleaner and let it soak a bit. It should be easy to clean after that.

If you are using paint creams or oils, you will clean your stencil during and after use. Use a paper towel moistened with a little bit of odorless mineral spirits. Lay your stencil on layers of newspaper, and rub gently to remove the paint residue.

Stencil Repair

If you do get damage, you can repair it temporarily by sandwiching the broken area in masking tape and recutting the shape with a craft knife.

Place the stencil on a piece of glass I have been known to just use a handy window and use the craft knife. The knife will glide over the surface of the glass and cut smoothly.

Storing Stencils

When you are done with your project, remove all the tape from the stencils and stack all your overlays together in the bag they came in. You can loosely roll them, but it is best if you store them flat.

Tip: Many stencilers place them on a piece of cardboard and slide them under the bed. They are out of the way, easily accessed, and the dust bunnies will keep them company!

Stencil Projects

Base Coat Basics

Okay, you all have walls, and most likely they are painted a neutral color such as the million and one shades of off-white that are on the market. It just so happens that the Diva's Definitive Technique for stenciling is most effective when done on a light neutral-color background. Is this your lucky day, or what?

The reason is this: In order for color to register in your brain as the color you think it should be, it needs to have a light-colored background to reflect it. To see what this is like, print a picture from your computer onto a colored piece of paper. The colors are not the same as they would be if printed on a white piece of paper.

Now don't go slamming the book closed because you have just painted your walls with the required 20 coats of paint to achieve that perfect shade of Hunter Green, and you wanted to paint ivy trailing across the walls. You can still do it.

If your walls are painted with a deep tone, you will need to do some test prints of your stencil design on that background color. Paint it out onto some cardboard and if you like the results, go ahead with your project.

If your wall is green and the green paints for your vines are too close to the color of the wall, or they clash, you will need to adjust the color of the stencil paint. Take a sample of your wall color to the craft store and find an acrylic color that will work.

If you don't, then first try giving each opening a light, but opaque, coat of either Taffy Cream or Sand as the first step. Then follow with the prescribed colors. This gives the colors a light base coat and the colors look correct.

Another option is to chose an entirely different color for your vines. You might consider using a metallic paint on a dark wall. The look is elegant!

If your paint is in good condition, and you're okay with the color, you don't need to repaint. But you should determine what kind of paint is on the walls, and the type of sheen so that you'll know what to expect when you start stenciling. Most homes are painted with flat latex-based paints, and you can stencil with acrylics or paint creams with no problems at all. If you have an older home that hasn't been painted in a long time, you may be dealing with an oil-based paint. If so, you won't be able to use acrylics successfully. I would recommend priming it and repainting with latex before I would hassle with oil-based paints.

Next, you'll want to figure out which type of sheen you are working with. If you are not certain, one good way to tell is to kiss the wall. And I don't mean a little peck on the cheek that you'd use for Great Aunt Gertrude. I'm talking a good ol' back seat of the Chevy at the drive-in movie kind of kiss! I know that sounds a bit off the wall . . . (ha ha) . . . but it works. Just be sure no one is watching you. If your lips kind of get stuck to the paint, then that's flat.

Flat finish is good if there are imperfections in the wall surface, because the light doesn't reflect off them and make them noticeable. However, on the other hand, it is not real scrubbable and it is really thirsty. It absorbs water quickly, and any water-based paint product that you apply will get sucked right into the finish. That means your stencil paint will be absorbed quickly into the base coat and you'll need to be a bit light-handed until you get the feel of it. If you want to do a faux finish on it, there is not much open time to work with before the finish is sucked into the base coat.

Be especially cautious if your home is brand new and you weren't around to choose the paint that was used. Contractors are not known for putting top quality paint on the walls, usually it is what is called "contractors grade." (Hmmmm . . .) In addition to that, they don't usually put on a very thick coat. So if you are going to invest your time and effort in a stenciling project, you may want a better quality base to stencil on. Your efforts here will be worth it.

The next sheen level up is what is called eggshell or satin matte. The term "eggshell" has nothing to do with the color of the paint. Eggshell is a finish, not a color. It is supposed to be like the finish that is on the shell of an egg. Some of the large paint store chains call it satin, some call it satin matte. Whatever they call it, I call it really nice. Giving it the ol' smackeroo test, your tongue will slide over the surface just a bit, and the wetness will not be absorbed as quickly as with flat paint. It is a joy to stencil on! The moisture in the stencil paint is not immediately sucked into the wall, and the finish feels really good to the touch. You've hit the jackpot!

You will probably be able to tell semigloss without kissing the wall, it is quite a bit shinier and the surface is fairly slick. People usually use semigloss in kitchens and bathrooms because it holds up to scrubbing. It can be a bit tricky to stencil on, because it isn't very absorbent. But just follow the Diva's Definitive Technique and you should have no problems.

Gloss enamel is a very shiny finish and you'll know if you have it. You'll want to use the peck on the cheek for this one! And have a towel handy! It is a very tight finish and not absorbent at all. Pay special attention to your technique. A very dry brush and ample drying time will be the key.

Surface Repairs

If there are any areas on the wall that need to be repaired, you should do that before you paint. Fill any holes with spackle and let it dry thoroughly. Then just take a damp terry towel and wipe the area. If you have texture on the walls, you will need to repair that too, or it will be noticeable.

"Texture?" you ask, "What is Texture?"

Wall Texture

I live in the Pacific Northwest, and any home that was built here in the past 35 years has textured walls. It seems to hold true all along the west coast. Houses just come with textured walls. You have to pay extra for smooth. I believe the reason for this is that houses were being built so fast they just didn't have the time it takes to do a smooth finish on the walls. They convinced people that this was something extra they were getting that was really wonderful. That is definitely a matter of opinion.

The textures range from smooth to stucco. The most common texture is called orange peel, because that is what it looks like; a uniform bumpy surface, like the skin of an orange. If you can't get smooth, this is the next best thing.

Then, there is what is called knock-down, or brocade texture. They spray on this wet plaster compound with an air gun—pile it on nice and heavy, then another guy comes along with a flat trowel and sort of smashes it down. The result is sort of like the surface of the moon, with flat parts and deeper craters. Then to make matters worse, they usually paint it with semigloss paint. You will lose some detail on this texture, so don't choose a design that is primarily made up of tiny, intricate parts.

When the contractors really don't want to do much to the wall, or someone has specifically requested it, they will just spray the stuff on and trowel it very lightly, making a rough stucco effect. If you have this type, you may want to choose designs that are bold in form, with large openings. It can be tough to get the paint through the stencil and onto the wall with any consistency.

If you are really unhappy with the texture on your walls, you can apply a skim coat to the surface, using fine drywall mud to fill in the gaps in the texture. It will be a project, that is for sure; but it is better than sanding it off.

Repairs on a textured wall are a bit tricky. You'll need to try to match the existing texture. There are spray cans of texture that you can get at paint stores, but know what texture you have before you buy it. You can get orange peel, knock down, and stucco sprays. Just spray the area and let it dry. It isn't meant for large areas, because it goes on rather inconsistently.

Any patched or repaired areas, textured or not, need to be primed before you paint. Be sure to get a can of PVA primer from the paint store. This primer will seal the surface of the patched area and will make the latex paint adhere properly to the patch.

If you don't prime, the patched area will be very noticeable because it will absorb the paint differently, This is especially important if you are going to apply any type of faux finish along with your stenciling. After the primer has dried, (it dries pretty fast), go ahead and paint the walls.

Tip: If all you have are teensy little holes that held the nail that Great Aunt Gertrude's picture was hanging from, I wouldn't bother filling them. After all, if you do fill them, how on earth will you figure out where it was hanging so you can put it back?

Working with Borders

Many stencils are designed to go around the top of a room. They can also be used to define linear areas within a room, such as around doors or windows. The general term for both types is "borders." However, one thing that I picked up from an art history class is that there is a difference between these.

In the hoity-toity art world, a wide band of pattern that runs horizontally around the top of a room is called a frieze. It is pronounced "freeze," not "frizay." (I wouldn't want you to appear to be uneducated, and suffer the ridicule of friends and family . . .) They can be used at many different locations on the wall, so use your own creativity where this is concerned. A frieze is most commonly used at the ceiling line; but I have used them effectively in the following ways: about 12" down from the ceiling, at chair rail height (between 30"–36" up from the floor), along the baseboard, and on the counter backsplash in the kitchen. I have even used them vertically to create stripes!

A border is a narrow band of pattern that typically runs around windows or doors, and borders an area both horizontally and vertically. Borders can also be used at chair-rail height and along the baseboard. They can be used to create frames around stenciled panel designs or to visually divide a wall into sections. Wherever they are used, they call attention to the area they define.

Frieze and border stencils come in all different lengths and styles. They also have a few other characteristics such as how they go together to form the border.

Continuous Frieze or Border

A continuous frieze or border is one that totally encircles the room at the top of the wall. There are no breaks in the design and it is important for the pattern to match up at the point where the last print meets the first print. If the frieze or border is loosely designed, you can shrink or stretch the space between repeats to fit your room.

Tightly Registered Frieze or Border

Some designs have no space between the repeats and are called tightly registered designs. Any fitting adjustments need to be done in the corners of the room.

Motif Frieze or Border

Motif friezes and borders can stand on their own as a motif, and can be positioned with equal amounts of space between the repeats, giving the room a balanced look.

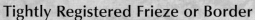

Project 1:
Continuous Frieze

Materials:

Supplies
Blue painter's tape
Paper plates
Paper towels

Stencil
Antique Roses

Paints
Avocado
Cranberry Wine
Dark Hause Green
Payne's Grey
Pink Chiffon
Raspberry

Stencil Brushes
¾" brushes (2)
1" brushes (4)

Laying Out Your Project

This project will show you how to run a continuous frieze around the top of your room. As I told you before, a continuous frieze is just that. Continuous. It doesn't have any break in the design. The Antique Roses design is made so that it has some flexibility built in. In other words, you can successfully leave a bit of space between the repeats without it looking disjointed. But how do you know how much space to leave? Read on, dear one. Diva will reveal the secret!

The groundwork for this type of frieze requires the use of the "M" word, MATH. I know many of us artsy types are mathematically challenged, so I had my daddy, who is a physicist of all things (can you believe it? Where did I come from!), write up this formula for all of us to use. It will make us appear very smart and save our diva reputations!

The first thing you will need to do is measure the room accurately. Use a tape measure to measure each wall separately and add the measurements together to get the total circumference of the room. Use a calculator. Just an itty bitty one will do. Write down the numbers. Don't rely on your memory; if it is anything like mine, it simply cannot be trusted.

Note: The total room measurement we'll call "T". In our example it is 506".

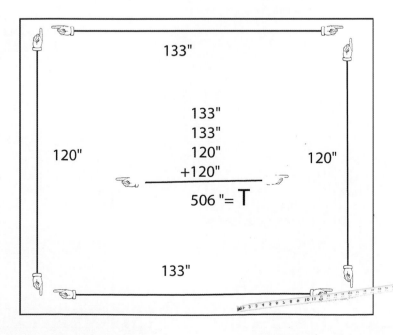

133"

133"
133"
120"
+120"
_____
506 "= T

120"   120"

133"

Next, measure the repeat length of the stencil. This is the horizontal distance between the registration holes at the top corners of the design. Ours measures 31". We'll call this number "R".

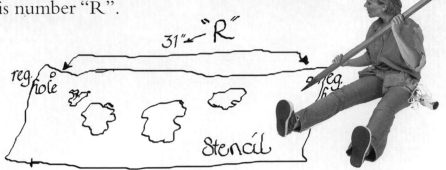

Divide "T" by "R", resulting in the number of repeats required to completely encircle the room. In this case it is 16 full repeats plus 0.32 of a repeat.

$$T \div R = Nx$$
$$506" \div 31" \approx 16.32 \text{ reps}$$

We'll call this number "N.x".

Now, the likelihood of "N" being a whole number without a remainder is pretty slim, if it is, go buy a lottery ticket! You are home free and won't have to make any adjustments to your stencil repeat. But if you do have a remainder, don't just ignore it. You will need to adjust the space between each repeat to get rid of the partial pattern. Just follow the formula that daddy wrote.

$$0.x \cdot R = TA$$
$$0.32 \cdot 31" \approx 9.92"$$

We will be dealing only with the remainder after this point, so we will call it "0.x". Convert the remainder to inches by multiplying "0.x" by the length of the repeat "R". This is the total amount in inches that will need to be adjusted out. We'll call this "TA".

To figure the space between each repeat, do the following:

$$TA \div N = A$$
$$9.92" \div 16 \text{ reps} = 0.623"$$
$$\text{or } 5/8"$$

Divide "TA" by "N" this will give you the amount of adjustment of each repeat. We'll call this "A". Ours turns out to be ⅝" space between each repeat.

How do you make the adjustment so that it is easily done and you don't have to measure the placement of each print when you are up on the ladder? It is very simple.

Go to your stencil and locate the registration hole at the top left corner of the first overlay. Use a ruler and measure over to the left of the hole the distance of "A", in our case ⅝". Use a permanent marker to make a tiny X. This will act as your new positioning point for spacing each repeat.

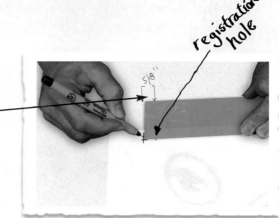

registration hole

You will still use the actual registration holes for aligning the overlays, but the spacing will be done by aligning this new point with the registration mark on the wall from the previous print.

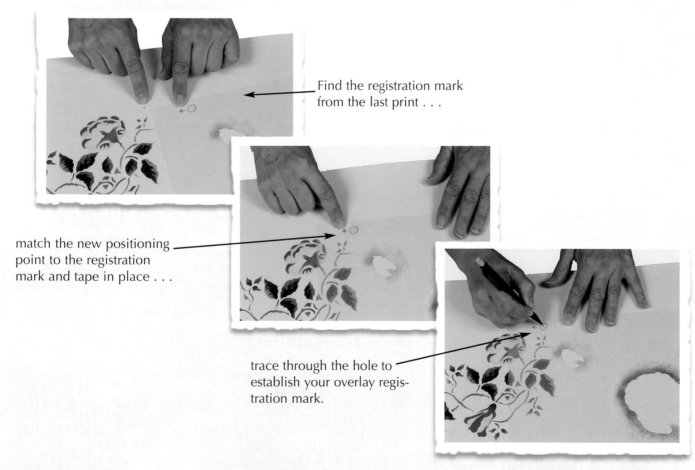

Find the registration mark from the last print . . .

match the new positioning point to the registration mark and tape in place . . .

trace through the hole to establish your overlay registration mark.

You will have to be the judge as far as how much adjustment is too much to add between each repeat. Because each design has its own flow, what may work for one pattern may not work for another. If there is a large remainder, and a long repeat length, you may find that the amount of adjustment is just too big a space to leave. In this case you can shrink the design by making the repeats closer together. Or you may need to just make the adjustment in the corners of the room.

Corners

The corners of your room often pose a problem when it comes to getting the stencil to bend into the corner and applying the paint neatly in that confined area. I circumvent this potential problem by creating a clean corner treatment that makes the job look much more professional.

In each corner of the room I run a strip of masking tape vertically down each wall. This creates a nice clean line and breaks the design in the corner. You may think that this will look unfinished, but the result is actually so neat and clean that the eye never picks up on the fact that there is a break in the pattern.

Note: Make sure the tape is parallel with the corner on both surfaces.

Determining Placement

You will want to begin your stencil pattern in the least noticed corner of the room, which is usually the corner above the door or at least on the same wall as the entry door. People don't tend to look there. This provides extra insurance just in case you did your math wrong! If you are running the border at the very top of the wall, you can use the top edge of the plastic as a guide. Just line up the top edge of the plastic with the ceiling, tape it in place, mark through your registration holes.

If your ceiling line is irregular, or you want to drop the border down a ways, then you will need to use a level to establish a guide line as shown below.

Measure down from the ceiling the desired amount and make a small pencil mark every so often.

Use your level to check your marks and make any adjustments to the marks.

Then you can line up your top edge of the Mylar with the guideline, and begin stenciling.

61

Stenciling

1 Load a 1" brush with Pink Chiffon according to the DDT (Diva's Definitive Technique on page 32). Stipple an even coat of color into all the cutouts on this overlay. Remember that several light coats are better than one heavy one!

Load a ¾" brush with Raspberry and stipple very lightly around the edges of each flower and a touch into the tiny buds. Remove the stencil.

3 Position overlay 3 by lining up the registration holes again. Load another 1" brush with Avocado and stipple the leaves and vines on this overlay.

Load a ¾" brush with Payne's Grey and add very light dimensional shading at the base and tips of the leaves and vines. Remove the stencil.

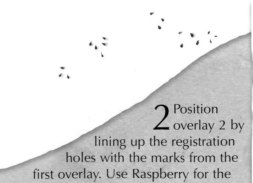

2 Position overlay 2 by lining up the registration holes with the marks from the first overlay. Use Raspberry for the rose detail. Load another 1" brush with Cranberry Wine and shade the detail; also use it for the tiny flower bud details. Remove the stencil.

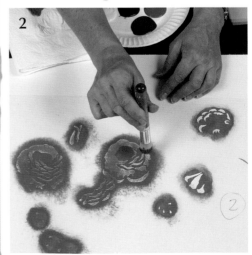

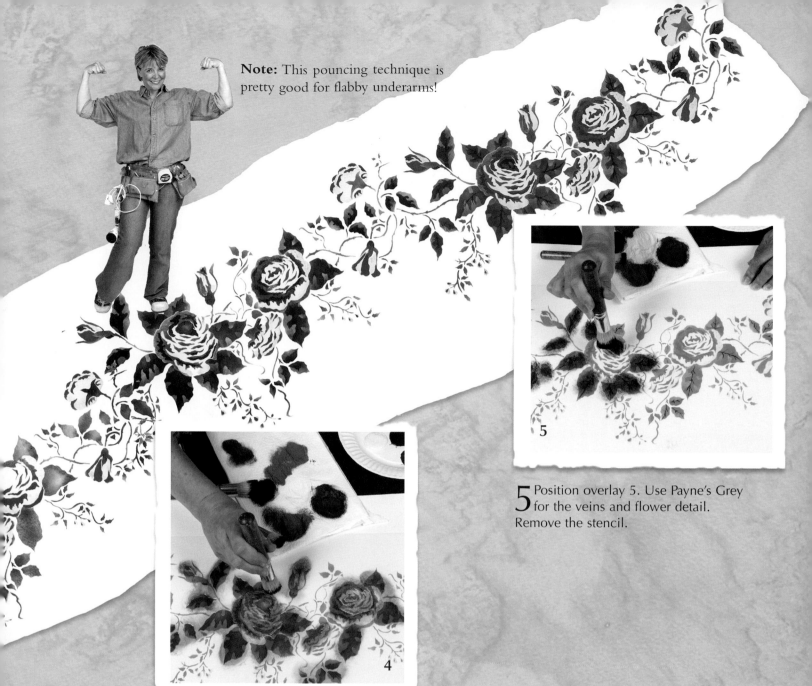

Note: This pouncing technique is pretty good for flabby underarms!

5 Position overlay 5. Use Payne's Grey for the veins and flower detail. Remove the stencil.

4 Position overlay 4 as before and load a 1" brush with Dark Hauser Green for the leaf detail an use Cranberry Wine for the rose detail. Remove the stencil.

Note: You have finished your first print; take down the stencil and Wall-Ahhhh! Let's hear it . . .OOOOOOHHH AAAAAhhhh! You've done beoootifully and are well on your way to Diva-dom! Don't stop now; you've got 15 more repeats to go!

Materials:
Supplies
Blue painter's tape
Paper plates
Paper towels

Stencil
Craftsman Rosehips Frieze

Paints
Avocado
Burnt Sienna
Celery Green
Heritage Brick
Hi-lite Flesh
Soft Black

Stencil Brushes
¼" brush
¾" brushes (3)
1" brushes (2)

Project 2:
Tightly
Registered
Border

Many lovely designs have tight registration between repeats, leaving no room to adjust each one evenly to fit in the room. Borders of this type are often associated with the Arts & Crafts movement during the 1920s. The images created during this time reflected nature in the style of Art Nouveau. The borders are very mechanical in their repetition, with one motif interlocking with the next. This leaves no space between each one for adjustment. All adjustments need to be done in the corners of the room. The thing that I like best about this type of repeat is that you don't have to do math to run the border. It is so easy, just treat each wall separately!

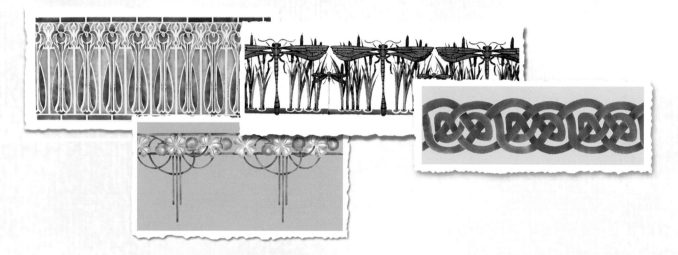

Preparation & Positioning

Because you are adjusting the design repeat at the corners of the room, you will need to establish a break in the design at the corners using masking tape. Just run a strip of blue tape down the walls in the corners of the room, getting the tape right into the corners. This will provide a nice clean corner and enable you to make the border flow beautifully. Your viewers will not even see the difference in the repeat!

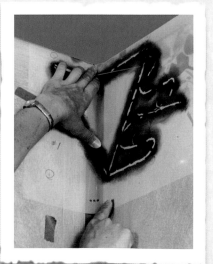

You will want to start your stenciling by positioning overlay 1 in a corner of the room, so that the stencil extends onto both walls. You may need to use a piece of tape at the top and bottom of the stencil to keep it held into the corner. Mark through the registration holes.

Stenciling

1 Begin stenciling by loading a 1" brush with Burnt Sienna. Unload the brush according to the DDT (Diva's Definitive Technique) on page 32, and stipple the entire overlay. If you are in the corner, stencil right over the tape.

Next, load a ¾" brush with Soft Black and add shading by pouncing just a couple times at each of the breaks in the vines. Remove the stencil.

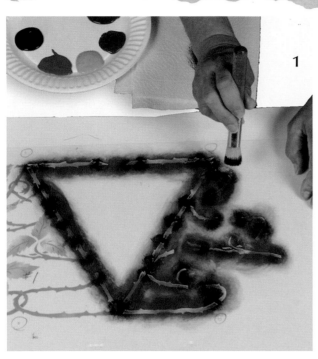

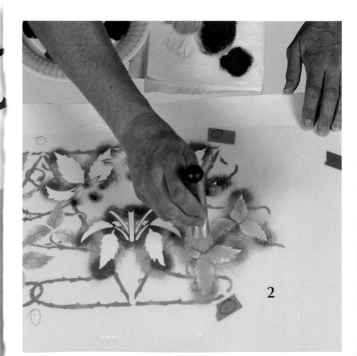

2 Position overlay 2 by lining up the holes with the marks from the first overlay. Load a ¾" brush with Celery Green and stipple color in the leaves.

Load another ¾" brush with Avocado and shade around the edges of each leaf lightly. Use a touch of Soft Black to lightly shade the base and tips of each leaf. For the flowers, use a ½" brush with Hi-lite Flesh.

Load a 1" brush with Heritage Brick and shade lightly around the edges and in the centers. Remove the stencil.

3 Position overlay 3 and use Heritage Brick for the round rose hips, shading around the edges with Soft Black. Use Burnt Sienna for everything else, shading the vines as before with Soft Black. Remove the stencil.

4 To do the next print, line up overlay 1 so that the holes on the left edge line up with the marks from the right end of the first print. Tape into place and repeat the instructions for all overlays. When you reach the end of that wall, continue your stenciling right up and over the tape. Keep going until all walls are done.

Notes: To move to the next wall, just wrap the stencil into the corner, apply your colors and move along across the wall. Continue in this manner around the room.

When you are finished, remove the tape and you have professional looking corners and no noticeable break in the design.

Defining Borders

A border is exactly what it says . . . a boundary. It serves to define an area by edging it with a band of decoration. A defining border needs to be fairly close to whatever it's defining, such as a door or window frame. Because the surrounding Mylar on a stencil is there to prevent you from inadvertently painting on your wall, there may be a rather wide space between the openings and the edge of the plastic. This could prevent you from getting your border close enough to the doorway. You can trim it off, just be very sure that you are not trimming away any registration marks or openings on the stencil.

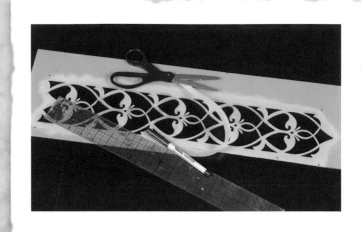

Lay your stencil on a flat surface and stack the overlays together, matching the registration holes. Check through each overlay to determine that you aren't going to cut anything off that shouldn't be cut off. Use a clear plastic grid ruler and line the grid up with the straight edge of the Mylar at the desired trim line. Mark the line with a permanent marker, keeping it straight. You don't want your border to go on crooked because you marked incorrectly. Use a pair of scissors to trim off the excess Mylar.

Making Miter Masks

When a border is used to frame an area, it is best to miter the corners where vertical and horizontal meet. This can be rather tricky, so I came up with my own solution called a miter mask. You can use a piece of printer paper, folded on the diagonal so that a 45° angle is formed. Trim off the excess, forming a triangle.

Fold the top of the triangle down and use the short edge against the molding of a door or window as shown on page 69.

Use the triangle if you are working on a portable project with free edges.

Position the stencil next to the door or window frame, and extending past the top intersection.

Tape mask in place along top edge of frame, covering up extended stencil.

Stencil according to directions in package, going right up over edge of mask. Don't go any further.

Remove stencil and mask, revealing mitered edge.

Place mask over the miter just painted and tape in place.

Position stencil along top edge of door frame and stencil.

YES!

TA-DAAAA!
A beoooty-ful mitered corner!

Project 3: Bordered Floor Cloth

Materials:

Supplies
24" x 36" piece of solid sheet vinyl
Carpenter's square
Foam roller
Foam roller refills
Paint conditioner
Paper plates
Paper towels
Pencil
Roller pan
Rubberized rug-backing paint

Supplies (cont.)
Scissors
Tape measure
Water-based primer sealer
Water-based varnish

Stencil
Moorish Border

Paints
Charcoal Grey
Khaki Tan
Sand (2 bottles)

Stencil Brushes
⅛" brush
1" brush

This floor cloth is a very easy and quick alternative to the traditional canvas type. It is stenciled on the back side of sheet vinyl flooring! You can usually find remnants at the home improvement stores or flooring shops. I found one that measured 3' x 10' for only $10. The surface is really smooth and fun to paint on. The Moorish Border stencil will be done around the edges of the floor cloth, so we will use the miter masks to do our corners.

1 Determine the size of your finished floor cloth, ours measures 24" by 36". Measure and mark the dimensions on the back of the vinyl, using a tape measure and a carpenter's square. The vinyl is soft and you can cut it carefully with scissors.

2 Apply a coat of water-based primer sealer to the back of the vinyl, using a foam roller. Allow it to dry.

3 In a clean roller pan, mix a bottle of Desert Sand acrylic with an equal amount of paint conditioner. Use a clean foam roller to apply an even base coat to the primed vinyl. Allow to dry.

4 Make four basic triangle miter masks.

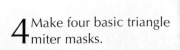

Stenciling the Short Sides

We will start on one short end of the floorcloth. Tape the masks onto the floor cloth as shown. Notice that the vinyl is sandwiched between the layers of the mask and one point of the triangle is right at the corner.

Tape the stencil along the short edge, overlapping the mask. Use Khaki Tan acrylic to stencil the border, going right onto the mask.

Use Charcoal Grey paint cream to shade the openings.

Remove the stencil and mask.

Tip: You can use rubberized rug-backing paint or a thin rug pad to keep the mat secure.

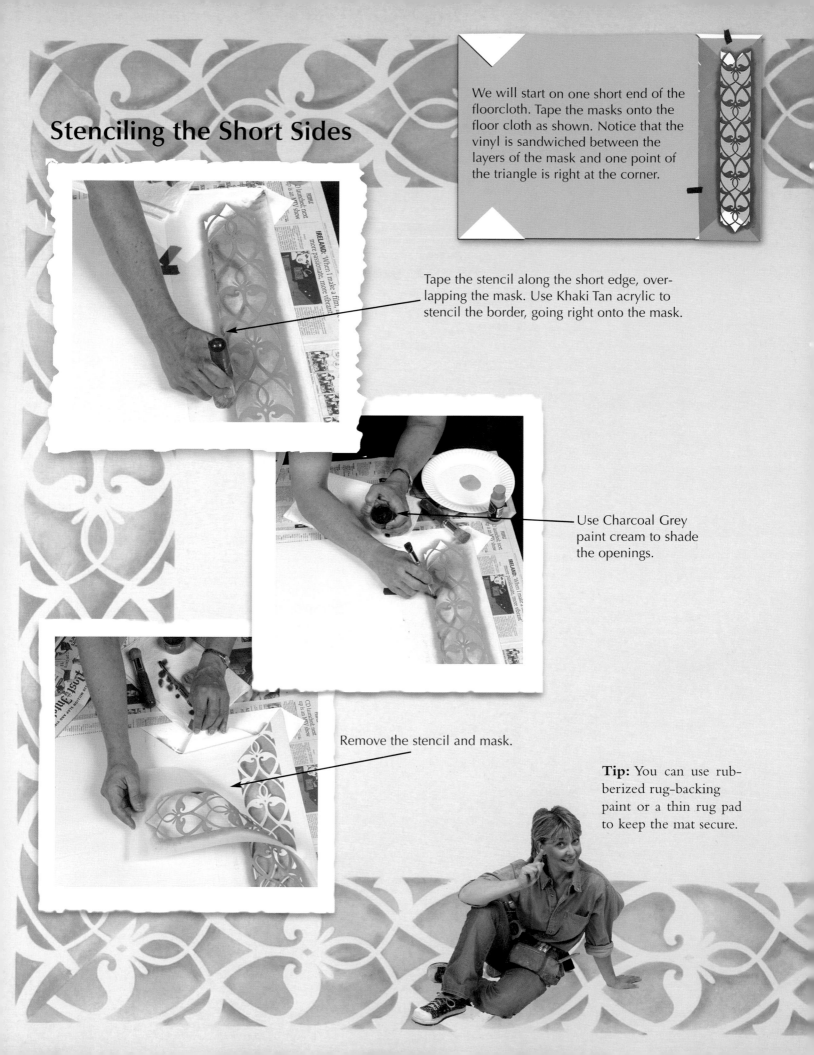

Positioning the masks for the long sides involves moving them to the short sides as shown. Tape them in place but be certain the tape doesn't get in the way.

Tape the stencil along the long side, overlapping the mask. Stencil again with Khaki Tan acrylic.

Use Charcoal Grey paint cream to shade the openings.

Remove the stencil and masks.

Apply four coats of water-based varnish to protect the decorative painting. Apply rubberized rug-backing paint on back of the mat.

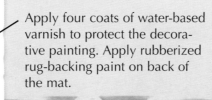

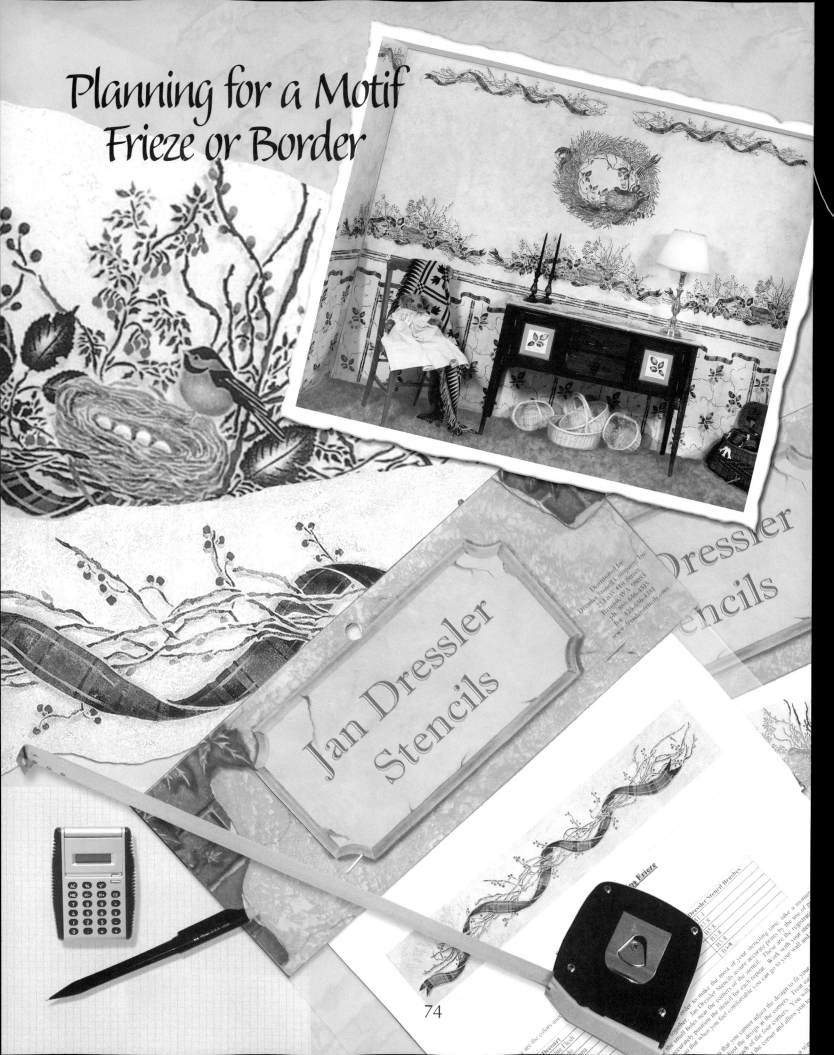

Planning for a Motif
Frieze or Border

Creative Applications of Friezes and Borders

If a traditional frieze or border is too weighty for your space, you can still get the border feeling by using a motif and spacing it out on the wall. The finished look will feel lighter and more spacious. Many lovely designs can be adapted in this way. A motif frieze is very easy to fit into a room. Most of your spacing relies upon your personal taste.

See how different spacing changes the look of this motif frieze?

The first step is to determine how close you want the motifs to be. One good way of determining this is to stencil out the design three times on butcher paper and cut the repeats apart. Tape them up on the wall and experiment with different spacing. Have a friend over to help, it's always a good excuse for a party. When you decide, measure the space between and use that as your determining factor.

Start by centering one motif on each wall and then calculating the space in between. Yes, you will need your calculator! Depending upon the length of the design and the size of your room, you will fit whatever number of repeats you wish in the remaining space.

Whatever you do, let your creativity shine through. Don't feel at all constrained by convention. Free thinking is encouraged, there are no boundaries!

Materials:
Supplies
Blue painter's tape
Paper plates
Paper towels
Practice paper
Scissors

Stencil
Secret Garden Ivy

Paints
Antique Teal
Payne's Grey
Taffy Cream

Stencil Brushes
1" brushes (3)

Project 4:
Random Ivy Border

Free-form Borders

Vines are great designs to use in a free-form manner to encircle the room. Ivy is one of the most popular vines because of its crisp, fresh look. Don't be limited in your color selection. Ivy can look like toile when done in blues or pinks. And what a unique room you would have!

A free-form border is very flexible and can be arranged to fit your unique space. It can be stenciled freely across a wall, or maybe just around the windows. Stencils are great because you can still get the look of a hand-painted freely flowing vine just by altering the pieces of vine that you use. You can use both sides of the plastic and get a different shaped vine each time. You can also tape off sections of the vine to use to tuck in here and there. You are free to use your imagination, but some planning is necessary in order to make the border look totally random.

If you are using both sides of the stencil, it makes the job easier if you can tell at a glance which side you are currently using. I write my name on the front side of the Mylar, using a permanent marker. If it reads correctly, then I'm using the front side. If it reads backward, I'm using the back side. It also helps when you are rotating the print, that way you will know which way to place your next overlay. I also circle the registration holes so that they are easily found. When building free-form, it also helps to use the blue painter's tape under your registration holes. It makes them easier to find on the wall.

Stenciling

1 Load a 1" brush with Taffy Cream and stipple a base coat in the center of the large leaves. You don't need to worry about the small ones, it gets covered up with the Antique Teal in the next step.

2 Load a 1" brush with Antique Teal and stipple the green around the edges of the leaves and all over the vines.

3 Load a 1" brush with Payne's Grey and add a touch of it at the base and tips of the leaves and along the vines. Remove the overlay.

Note: This is what the Payne's Grey does . . . it makes the leaves look so rich and sophisticated. This ain't your mama's stenciling!

4 Position overlay 2 and use Payne's Grey for the leaf veins. You're done!

Planning Your Layout

This illustration shows how you build with free-form vines. You can get a good idea how your vine will look by stenciling out on paper two or three repeats from both the front and back of each section of ivy. You can cut out pieces and tape them together on the wall. Then you can stand back and see what shapes emerge! Then you can rearrange the pieces so that the shapes disappear.

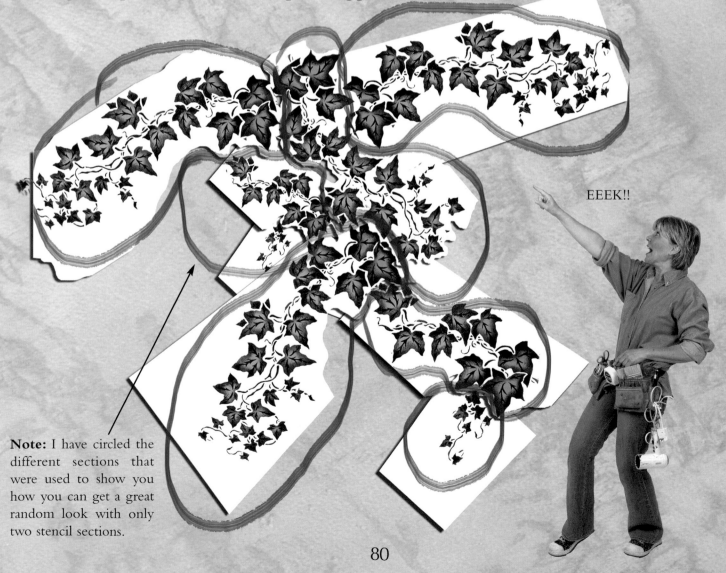

EEEK!!

Note: I have circled the different sections that were used to show you how you can get a great random look with only two stencil sections.

When you are ready to stencil, you can leave the pattern up and remove each piece of paper after you have positioned your stencil. That way you will be sure that your finished look is just like your plan.

Remove the paper from under the stencil and off you go!

Stencils can be used to create allover repeats that actually look like wallpaper. And just like wallpaper, there are many effects you can get from an allover repeat. You can combine the allover repeats with simple faux finishes that complement the stencil design. All you need to do is decide what look you want. There are many to choose from.

Your pattern does not have to go from floor to ceiling. It can just cover the wainscot, or the area above the wainscoting. You can do just one wall or the entire room. Once again, the choice is yours and your individuality has room for expression!

Allover repeats are made by stenciling rows and columns of repeats. You line up the repeats by matching the registration holes in the corners of the stencil. It all sounds simple enough and in a perfect world, you'd just start at one end of the wall and work your way across. Everything would turn out perfectly. That's what I thought. Then I tried it.

I can tell you this from experience; allover repeats have their own set of interesting quirks. If not done properly, the design can telescope as you work your way across the wall and some of the repeats at the far end will amazingly have more and more space between them, others will have less, and it ends up looking like one of those mirrors in the funhouse!

So after repainting a couple times, I came to the conclusion that I needed to narrow my margin for error. I could do that by starting in the center of the wall, establishing a perfectly straight vertical row, and then establish a perfectly horizontal row, near the middle of the wall. Once those two foundation rows were set, all I'd need to do was fill in the four qaudrants, leaving a lot less room for problems. I tried it and it worked!

Note: The next four projects are done using this concept.

83

Project 5:

Materials:
Supplies
Blue painter's tape (2" wide)
Paper plates
Paper towels

Stencil
Stone Block Wall, small

Paints
Charcoal Grey Paint Cream
Khaki Tan Acrylic

Stencil Brushes
¼" brush
1" brush

Jan Dressler Stencils

Stone Block Wall

This repeat is formed by stenciling in the cracks between the blocks. You will do this first and add your visual texture afterward by sponging or applying a light French wash as shown on pages 88–89. Let's start with the basic grid, using the Stone Block Wall stencil.

Forming the Basic Grid

Start with the Right Tools

3' Carpenter's level
Heavy thread
Metal washer or key
Pencil
Push pins
Tape
Tape measure

Making and Using a Plumb Bob

Measure off 8' of heavy thread or light string. Tie one end to the heavy washer and tie a loop in the other end.

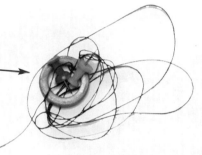

I'm just plumb crazy over Plumb Bob!

Anchor your push pin at the top of the wall, slip the loop over it and let the weight find it's center. You can tape the thread to the wall at the top and at the bottom. You can just leave it there if it is thin enough, and work right on top of it.

Or you can make tick marks with a pencil beside the string and take it off the wall. This is your vertical plumb line, and you will use it to line up your vertical row of prints.

Note: No matter which allover design you use, you will start the same way. You will treat each wall separately and start in the middle of the wall with your vertical plumb line.

Vertical Grid Row

1 Start at the bottom of the wall and position your stencil so that the bottom edge of the design rides along the top of the baseboard, and the registration holes along the right side line up directly on top of the thread. Tape the stencil in place, and mark through all registration holes with a pencil. Use a 1" brush loaded with Khaki Tan and stencil the entire repeat.

2 Remove the stencil and reposition it above the first print, matching the bottom pair of holes on the stencil with the top set of marks from the first print. Lineup the pair of registration holes on the right edge with the vertical guideline as before.

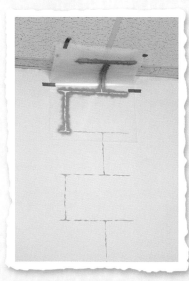

3 Stencil, and continue this process until you reach the top of the wall.

Note: You probably won't have a full repeat at the top, but that is okay. Just stencil right up to the ceiling line.

Horizontal Grid Row

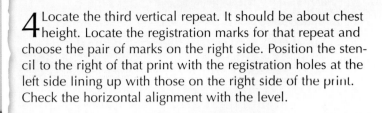

4 Locate the third vertical repeat. It should be about chest height. Locate the registration marks for that repeat and choose the pair of marks on the right side. Position the stencil to the right of that print with the registration holes at the left side lining up with those on the right side of the print. Check the horizontal alignment with the level.

5 Mark through the registration holes and stencil as before. Repeat the process across the wall to the right and to the left of the vertical row.

6 Fill in the quadrants and you will have no problems with the repeats lining up perfectly.

Note: If you are doing an entire room, finish all walls before adding the visual texture.

87

French Wash

If you are not going to do the wash on your ceiling, you will need to protect the edge of the ceiling at the top of the wall. Use 2"-wide tape so that you have more protection from errant swipes. Tape off your woodwork also. This is really the most time-consuming part of it all.

Materials:
Absorbent drop cloth
Blue painter's tape (2" wide)
Bucket
Natural sea sponges (2)
Paint conditioner solution
Tan interior latex, eggshell finish
Rubber gloves
Water

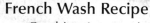

Drop your sponges into a bucket of clean water and let them soak. Keep the bucket handy, so that you can keep your sponges from drying out. A sponge will be ruined if paint is allowed to dry in it.

French Wash Recipe

Combine 1 part paint, 1 part water, and 1 part paint conditioner. It should be the consistency of whole milk. Mix it with gloved hands, your fingernails will be a lovely shade of khaki if you don't.

1 Wring the water out of the sponges. One will be for the paint and one will be used to dampen your wall and keep your edges from drying.

Dunk one sponge into the wash. Hold it well down inside the bucket while you squeeze it so that you don't squirt wash all over the place. You want to have a well-wrung sponge. Nothing wet and drippy. Wipe off your hands with the sponge before you go to the wall, drips are hard to work into a finish!

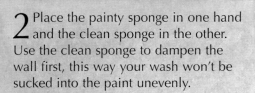

2 Place the painty sponge in one hand and the clean sponge in the other. Use the clean sponge to dampen the wall first, this way your wash won't be sucked into the paint unevenly.

Now use the painty sponge to wash the wall, using small "C" strokes, using the clean sponge to soften any hard edges. Fade out the beginning edge by going over it with the clear sponge. Work quickly; dampening the oncoming area with the clear sponge and then washing it with the painty one.

3 Reload your sponge as needed, wringing it out well. Keep your damp sponge clean by rinsing it out occasionally in the bucket. But keep moving.

Continue around the room. Blend in your starting point and you're done! Throw your sponges into the bucket of water before you collapse.

When you are done with all the walls, lie down in the middle of the room and relax, you deserve it!

Visual Texture and Dimensional Shading

To create the illusion of stone, visual texture and illusion need to be added. You can use the sponge with some full-strength paint on it to pat in some additional textural effects to random blocks. Work your way across the wall. Remember that it doesn't have to be evenly applied.

1 Give the blocks some depth and dimension by shadowing with Charcoal Grey paint cream. After removing the skin from the top of the paint, load a ¼" brush.

Crumple up one paper towel and hold it in your left hand. Unload the brush by swirling it into the paper towel. Keep the towel in your hand along with the pot of Charcoal Grey paint cream.

2 You will apply the paint, using a scrubbing motion. Really scrub the brush, just above the grout line at the bottom of each block and just inside the grout line along one edge. Work your way along the wall shadowing each block. It will look really dark and icky at this point, so don't panic. We will take care of that in a moment with the mineral spirits.

3 When you're done with the wall, take another paper towel and add a very small amount of mineral spirits to it. Squish the towel together to distribute the solvent.

Then rub it gently along the lines of shadow, fading them so that they look realistic. It is totally amazing how this transforms the wall.

TA-DAAA!!!

Tip: You may go back and add random cracks or hand-paint holes in the "stones." Add as much embellishment as you wish, the wall will look great!

91

Project 6:
Damask Wallpaper Repeat

Materials:

Supplies
Blue painter's tape (2" wide)
Drop cloth
Faux glazing liquid
High-density sponge roller
Paper plates
Paper towels
Plastic spoons
Roller pan
Rubber gloves

Stencil
Damask Wallpaper Repeat, large

Paint
Khaki Tan

For French Wash
Natural sponges (2, large and full)
Tan interior latex, eggshell finish
Paint conditioner (1 gallon)

For Easy Pearly Faux Finish
Iridescent Pearl acrylic (1 pint)
Natural sponge
Paint bucket
Utility bucket (5 gal)

An elegant Damask repeat can really dress up a wall, especially when it is applied on top of a beautiful pearlized faux finish. Don't let the "Faux" scare you, I wouldn't recommend it if it wasn't just as easy as pie!

When you use pearlized paints, their impact is dependent upon the reflection of light in the room. If you have low light you may need to increase the amount of pearl paint that you apply; but be aware that when you turn on the lights, there will be more reflection. Start with a light application, turn on the lights and see if you need more. If you feel that there is too much reflection, cut it back by sponging with the full-strength base French wash color. This will tame down the pearl finish.

French Wash

You will first want to apply a French Wash according to the French wash directions on page 88–89, using Tan interior latex paint. Do your entire area and leave the drop cloth in place.

Pearly Drifts

To give you an idea of the scale of the drifts, imagine a rectangle on your wall that reaches vertically from floor to ceiling and horizontally between 6'–8'. Your airy drift of pearly-ness will span from the top-left corner to the bottom-right corner. Then you will go straight up to the top and do it again in the next imaginary rectangle.

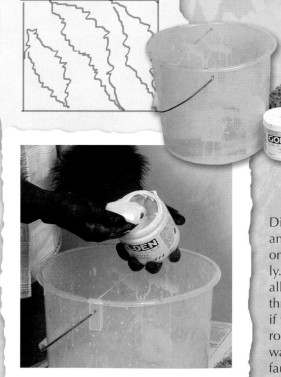

Pearly Paint Recipe

Scoop the Iridescent Pearl acrylic into a bucket. Depending upon the size of your room, you will probably use at least half the pint of paint. Mix about 3 tablespoons of paint conditioner into it and add the same amount of water. Don't get it too thin, you want to have some intensity to the drifts.

Dip your sponge into the pearly paint and wring it out. Loosely pat the sponge on the wall, going downward diagonally. Keep some space within the drift, allowing the washed wall to peek through. Continue around the room and if your drift starts near the corner of the room, just continue it onto the next wall. This is the final step in the easy faux. Now you can stencil.

W ith a large single-color design print like this, it is faster to use a sponge roller for the application. I also like to make it look faded and "old world." To do this, you will want to add a small amount of glaze liquid to the paint. However, be aware that this adds a bit more liquid to the paint and it will be a bit more difficult to control.

Mix your paint and the glaze liquid in the ratio of 1 bottle of paint to twice the amount of glaze. Use a plastic spoon to mix the solution in the paint tray, working to mix it well.

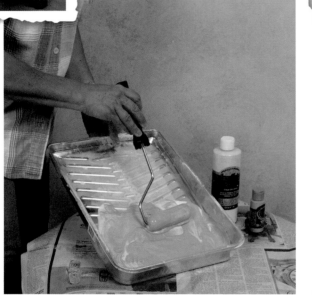

Follow this method for loading your roller and you should not have any problems:

Use a clean, dry sponge roller on a handle and roll it into the paint solution. Roll it on the deck of the pan to unload the bulk of paint, You will want a nice even imprint that leans more to the dry side.

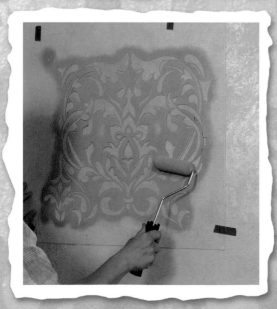

Start at the outside edges of the stencil, applying a light touch and short strokes. Work your way across the design. Don't press too hard so that the paint goes under the stencil. A light touch is all it takes.

Follow the instructions on page 85 for making your grid and your finished results will be perfectly lovely!

There are so many other color options to choose from with this design. Here are some ideas:

You can also use a tone-on-tone effect by going a shade darker or a shade lighter than the base color.

It is very effective to use a satin varnish for the stencil on top of your flat or eggshell latex paint. This produces a very subtle pattern that reflects light beautifully.

Metallic luster paint is lovely as well. The only limit is your imagination!

Project 7:

Mirror Image Wallpaper Repeat

Materials:

Supplies
Blue painter's tape (2″ wide)
Carpenter's level
Faux glazing liquid
Pencil
Roller pans (3)
Rubber gloves
Sea sponges (3)

Stencil
Florentine Damask, large

Paints
Black Plum
Emperor's Gold
Irridescent Bronze

This project covers a large area and creates a total repeat from four prints of the stencil. It produces a very dramatic and exotic effect. The Florentine Damask can take on a very light and airy look with pearl and silver on a white background or a very sultry and exotic look using a pumpkin colored base coat and stenciling in Venetian Gold and Bronze. Any way you go with this fabulous design, you'll be the talk of the town!

A very exotic look can be achieved by using metallic paints and natural sponges to stencil with. The reflection of the metallic and the textural effect of the sponging combine to create a beautiful finish. You can mix the metallic acrylics with glazing liquid to help cut some of the reflective quality.

Mix the paint and glaze equally in three separate paint trays, with a sponge for each color.

Tip: Be sure that you have soaked your sponges well and have a bucket of water handy to rinse them occasionally. Wring them out thoroughly, then dip one side into the glaze mixture. Blot it on the paint tray and have newspapers handy for additional blotting if necessary. You don't want to have too much paint that may run under the stencil.

Pat the sponge very gently directly down on top of the stencil, don't rub at all.

Apply one color at a time starting with the lightest colors.

When you are done, use a hair dryer to dry the paint and the stencil before you reposition it for the next print.

97

Stencil Placement

When using a very large repeat design like this one, it is important that you have the focal points of the repeat at the desired place on your wall. As this repeat develops, different elements make themselves evident. One focal point is the four radiating spiky stems and another is the four flowers, These elements are very strong and you should plan to place them in the appropriate places. So with that in mind, your vertical row doesn't have to begin at the bottom of the wall. It can begin anywhere and you can work upward and downward from that initial print.

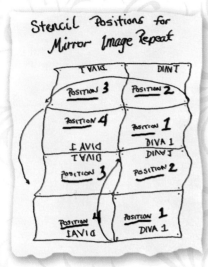

The trickiest part about working with this design is to keep the orientation of the stencil correct. After you get going with it, it becomes very obvious which way the stencil goes. The basic grid layout is virtually the same, but you will be manipulating the stencil as you go.

First Vertical Row

Position 1: Locate the copyright information on the stencil. The first print will be positioned so that the printing reads correctly, and so that one vertical edge of the Mylar is lined up with your plumb line. Sponge on the colors, one at a time, and dry the stencil and paint with a hair dryer before you move on.

Position 2: Flip the stencil over vertically so that the copyright information is at the top of the sheet, upside down and backward. Position it directly above or below the first print, match the holes in the Mylar with the set of marks from the first print. Sponge on your colors and dry the image. Remove the stencil. You have now formed a mirror image of the single print. Continue flipping vertically until you reach the ceiling.

First Horizontal Row

Position 3: Match your stencil with the third vertical repeat and flip it to the left (like turning a page in a book), so that the copyright information is still on the bottom of the stencil but it reads backwards. Match the registration holes along the right edge of the stencil with the marks from the left side of the vertical print. Tape in place, and stencil as before. Mark through the registration holes and dry the print.

Position 4: Flip the design up vertically completing the four part repeat. The copyright information will read upside down and backward. Match the registration holes and sponge on your colors. Dry and remove the stencil. Continue flipping and sponging until your wall is complete.

The effect is absolutely gorgeous!

Materials:

Supplies

Blue painter's tape
Carpenter's level
Clear plastic grid ruler
Craft knife
Graph paper
Metal ruler
Paper plates
Paper towels
Pencil
Permanent marker
Piece of glass for cutting surface

Stencil

#113L, M or S

Note: You can also enlarge and photocopy the pattern on page 127, and trace onto 24" square of Mylar or laminating film (available mail order or at laminating supply companies).

Paint

Any color desired, acrylic

Stencil Brush

1" or larger brush

Project 8:
Checkerboard
Wallpaper Repeat

An allover pattern of checkers is so fresh and can have so many different looks. You paint on the squares, using your wall color as the base tone. It can provide a wonderfully serene background when done in a tone-on-tone color scheme. It can look whimsical when done in multi-colors. It can be very graphic with high-contrast colors, soft in pastels on white, elegant in metallics on a faux finish background . . . it is just one of those universal patterns that I simply love!

If You Want to do the Multicolored Version, Use Four Colors:
Cadmium Yellow
True Blue
Napthol Red
Festive Green

Rows One and Three
Use alternating squares of Cadmium Yellow and Napthol Red.

Rows Two and Four
Use alternating squares of Festive Green and True Blue.

Copy the Checkerboard Allover Repeat Pattern on page 127 and enlarge it as desired. My squares measure 3". You can use graph paper or just mark out a grid of 1" squares, using a see-through grid ruler. It is very important that you get your squares straight, so spend the time now and your job will go much smoother.

Making the Stencil

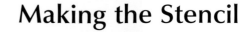

Using a permanent marker with a fine tip and your ruler, transfer the drawing to Mylar, including the dashed lines outside of the large squares. These are used for placement, and are very important.

Place the Mylar on a sheet of glass and cut out the squares, using a metal ruler and craft knife.

Note: Take a look at the stencil. You will see two parallel rows of squares. When you paint through the squares, it will create the first and third rows of checkers.

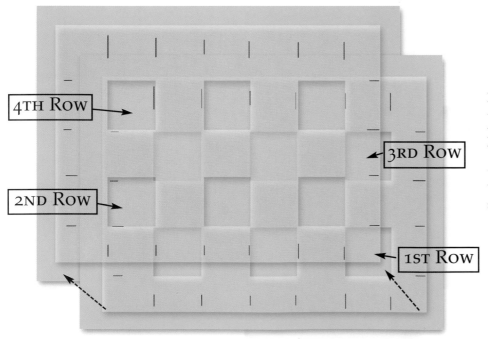

4TH ROW

3RD ROW

2ND ROW

1ST ROW

Note: By shifting the stencil up and to the left, you will notice that by lining up the dashed lines along the bottom and right side with the checkers from the first print, you will be able to accurately fill in the second and fourth rows of checkers.

Stenciling

1 Establish your basic grid and position your stencil horizontally at the bottom of the wall. Get your checks as close as possible to the baseboard.

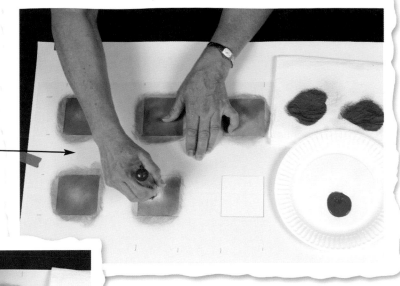

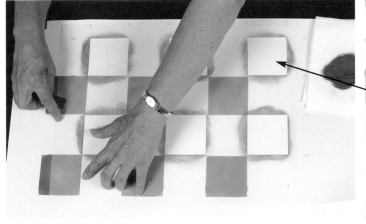

2 Use Forest Green to stencil your first section of checkers. Use a circular motion to swirl over each square, working for even coverage.

3 Shift your stencil up one row and to the right, lining up the dashed lines along the bottom and left end with the first section of painted checks. This creates the second and forth rows of checkers. Stencil the squares.

4 Continue in this manner until all is done.

T rompe l'oeil . . . one of the most mispronounced words in the decorative painting dictionary. Once more, the Diva will inform you so's you won't appear to be lacking in foreign languages. Tromp Loy . . . that's it. That's how you say it. Easy huh? What does it mean? Oh, it means to trick the eye. Oh, and it's French.

Trompe l'oeil artwork is very realistic, so realistic that your mind is fooled into thinking, for just a moment, that the painted object is real. It is fun for the artist and fun for the viewer. I enjoy designing and stenciling trompe l'oeil more than anything else.

My entryway had a blank wall at the end and I chose to create the illusion of an extended hallway.

This guest suite in a condo in Hawaii was just off the living room and the large bare wall behind the beds was overwhelming. I added this trompe l'oeil view from a balcony along with parrots and stenciled headboards to visually open up the room. My son thought we had remodeled!

Trompe l'oeil is very effective in room settings, where the three-dimensional fixtures within the room add to the illusion of reality. Choose a setting where a viewer is just passing through and for a brief second, his eye is caught off guard by the painted illusion. The goal of trompe l'oeil is to fool the eye of the viewer, and make them look twice. If you succeed in that, then you know you have mastered the art of trompe l'oeil.

Stenciling

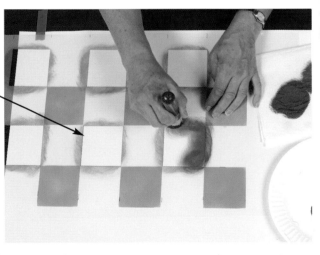

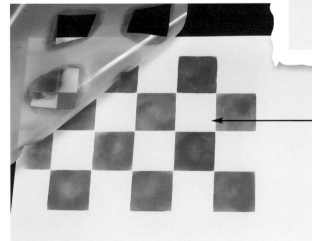

You don't need a lot of trompe l'oeil, in fact sometimes just a single tiny element will do. I know of someone who stenciled a wreath on their kitchen wall and it fools people every time! The wine rack, shown at right, is in my own home and it looks so real, my mom thought it was a new addition to the house!

What makes trompe l'oeil successful? There are several requirements:

- The object needs to be as realistic as possible. Some stencils that are advertised as trompe l'oeil actually have a cartoonish quality to the design, with sort of a whimsical look to the image. That is not truly trompe l'oeil. You wouldn't think it was a real object. It's cute, but not true trompe l'oeil.

- The object needs to look solid. Your stenciling technique cannot be pale or light handed.

- The image must be in proper perspective. If a pot is designed to sit on the floor line, placing it at waist height or above will destroy the perspective, and the resulting print will not be convincing.

- The image must be of proper scale for its position within the scene. Again, it must be convincing.

- The object must have dimension, achieved by highlights and cast shadows, and the shadows need to be consistent and realistic.

- The object must be grounded. Don't have a floating topiary on your wall. If it is meant to look real, use a stencil for a pot stand to raise it up from the baseboard.

How do you stencil a trompe l'oeil design? There are some tried-and-true methods that I will show you, using the lovely combination of stencils shown at right.

Project 9:
Trompe L'oeil Niche

Materials:

Supplies
Blue painter's tape
Natural sea sponge
Odorless mineral spirits
Paint conditioner
Paper plates
Paper towels

Stencils
Stone Window
Stone Niche

Paints
Charcoal Grey paint cream
Ebony Black paint cream
Khaki Tan acrylic

Stencil Brushes
¼" brushes (2)
1" brush

M any homes that I have stenciled, and lived in for that matter, have had a small blank wall right as you come in the front door, where a hall tree might stand, but the space is always too small for anything with dimension. It is the perfect place for a trompe l'oeil niche. The location of the design on the wall is the most critical part of the project. This design has built-in perspective and needs to be placed at the correct height in order for the illusion to work.

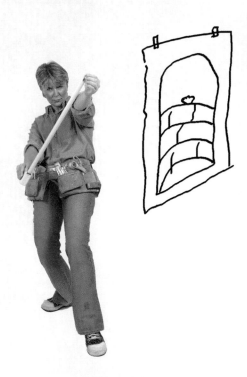

The perfect viewing distance for the niche is from 6' to 8' away. Any further than that and the niche floor starts to tip down. To determine the placement of your niche, you may need a friend. If you haven't got one, you're in bigger trouble than I thought, but you're not dead in the water.

For those of you with a friend, have them stand next to the wall in question and hold up the first overlay of the stencil, starting with the center shell at about eye level. Now, you step back to the most common viewing distance for general traffic. Have your friend move the stencil up or down until it looks good from where the most people will see it. Pay close attention to the floor of the niche. If you need to have the stencil viewed from further away than recommended, then you should locate the niche lower on the wall. You may need to stencil something inside the niche that will effectively take away the floor perspective.

Now those of you without friends, you can tape the stencil to the wall and step back, walk up and change it, step back. You know the drill, you're used to being a hermit! (I personally don't have any friends either, so don't feel bad!) I enjoy my own company so much, anyone else spoils the party!

Stenciling the Niche

1 Position overlay 1 on the wall so that the little pointy part of the shell is at eye level. Use your carpenter's level to be certain that the niche is straight on the wall. Tape it in place and mark through the registration holes.

Tip: The little shell mask in the center of the niche is kinda floppy. You can secure it to the wall by making a "tape hole" in it. Use scissors and very carefully cut a small hole in the Mylar of the shell mask. Then put a piece of blue painter's tape over it, pressing it to the wall. It will stick and the floppy mask will stay put!

2 Prepare your sponge by soaking it in a bucket of clear water. On a paper plate, squeeze out a spiral of Khaki Tan and add a spiral of paint conditioner. Wring out the sponge really well and dip it into the plate, smooshing it around. It should not be sloppy or wet.

3 Sponge color onto the blocks, and lightly in the arched area at the top. Gently pat the sponge directly onto the stencil, not moving it around at all. Toss the sponge into the water to keep it from getting ruined. Use a hair dryer to dry the sponged area.

4 Use a ¼" brush and Charcoal Grey paint cream to outline the blocks and the arched area. Add a touch to the bottom edges of the pointy part of the shell in the center of the niche. Use a paper towel to soften the shading of the blocks. Remove the overlay.

5 Overlay 2 and 3 are on the same piece of Mylar. If you want, you can cut them apart. Either way, line up each one, using its own pair of registration holes. Position overlay 2 first, and use Charcoal Grey paint cream shaded with Ebony Black paint cream for the long skinny openings fanning out from the center. Use Charcoal Grey paint cream on the upper edges of each of the shells side scallops and on the inner-long edges of the upper scallops. Remove the stencil.

6 Position overlay 3, and use Charcoal Grey paint cream to outline the center section of the shell design and on the lower long edges of the side scallops. Add a touch of Ebony Black paint cream to the edges of the scallops on the right side of the design. Use a deeper concentration of Charcoal Grey paint cream for the flute detail, adding a touch of Ebony Black paint cream to some of the flutes on the right side of the arch. Remove the stencil.

Stone Window

Y ou will surround the Niche with the stone window. Normally you would start with the big blocks on overlay A1. But because we are fitting the window to the niche, you will start with the inner blocks on A2. The registration holes will line up with those at the sides of the niche.

Load your sponge as before and pat color onto the blocks. Dry it with a hair dryer, remove the stencil and position overlay A1 with the large arch of blocks. Repeat the sponging. Dry again.

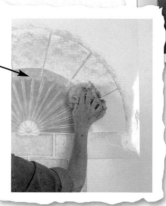

B2, the skinny blocks that form the sides and the bottom-front edge of the window, will be positioned at the left side of the niche. The overlay will be matched to the registration holes at the left-lower edge of Section A, right side up with the copyright information reading correctly, and the word "TOP" at the top of the design. Sponge like before, and dry it with the hair dryer. Flip it over along the inner edge, like turning a page in a book, and repeat the sponging. Follow with B1.

Finishing Touches

Add a shadow below the inner shell ornament, using Charcoal Grey paint cream and a touch of Ebony Black paint cream.

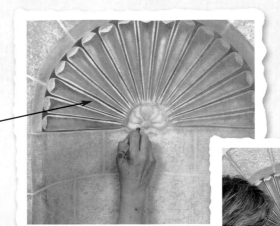

Shadow the bottom edges of the lower blocks and the lower edges of the side blocks with Charcoal Grey paint cream. Smooth out the application by rubbing with the paper towel.

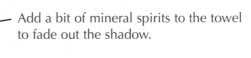

Add a bit of mineral spirits to the towel to fade out the shadow.

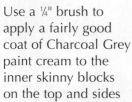

Use a ¼" brush to apply a fairly good coat of Charcoal Grey paint cream to the inner skinny blocks on the top and sides of the arch. Add Some Ebony Black paint cream to the top-inner blocks and along the right side, which will be in shadow. Smooth out the application with a paper towel. Let the paint cure for a few days and then you can add more shadows within the arch. I'll show you how later on.

Project 10:
Acanthus Vase

Materials:
Supplies
Blue painter's tape
Paper plates
Paper towels

Stencil
Acanthus Vase

Paints
Antique White acrylic
Charcoal Grey paint cream
Ebony Black paint cream
Khaki Tan acrylic

Stencil Brushes
⅛" stencil brushes (2)
1" stencil brushes (2)

Layering Images

It is very effective for the trompe l'oeil illusion if you have something inside the niche to focus on. A stone vase is a good focal point. Positioning the vase is very important. You need to remember that it is an object with volume. So it can't be pushed back against the back of the niche. It wouldn't have room, and your trompe l'oeil would not be convincing.

In order for the vase to look real, it must have a solid coverage of paint so that you can't see the background image through the foreground image. The trick to layering images within a scene is to give the overlying image a base coat of a light neutral acrylic. This will effectively block out the background images and prevent them from ghosting through.

Now, I've done this a lot, and believe me, even if you are putting a darker color over a lighter image, any contrast within the background, like the mortar between the blocks in the niche, will ghost through the overlying image. So save yourself some time, and listen to Diva. Apply your base coat nice and solid and everything will be lovely. I wouldn't steer you wrong!

1. Center the base of the vase platform, on overlay 1 in the niche, about 1½" up from the front edge of the bottom blocks. Tape it in place. Mark through your registration holes.

2. Properly load a 1½" brush with Antique White, and stipple a coat of it through all of the stencil openings.

Dry the paint with a hair dryer and repeat the base-coating until it is opaque. It is quite fortunate for you that this antique white is one of the colors used in the vase itself, so it serves both as the blocking color and the base color of the object. This must be your lucky day!

Shading

The shading is the most important part of this design and for all trompe l'oeil. It creates contrast within the image to make the object look three-dimensional. Areas on an object that are closest to you appear brighter in color and those receding areas appear darker as if in shadow. To form your darker areas, you will use the Charcoal Grey paint cream right on top of the acrylic base coat. Keeping the stencil in place while you do the shading creates a photographic edge—a quality that is very difficult to achieve without a stencil. It is critical to keep your shading smooth and realistic.

You want the shading to blend naturally into the vase, so you will be using the paper towel, and maybe even a touch of mineral spirits, to fade in the shading. Be careful not to use too much mineral spirits because it will take off all the Charcoal Grey. I usually just hold my wadded up paper towel tight on the spout of the can and tip it over once. There should just be a bit of dampness on the towel. Then I sort of squish it around so that it distributes into the towel. I can then rub the area with the towel and get a very soft shadow.

1 To add volume to the vase, use the ⅛" brush and dip it into the pot of Charcoal Grey paint cream. Unload it on the paper-towel blotter and sketch or scrub the paint on along the edges of the stencil. You can use a circular scrubbing motion to work the translucent paint onto the surface. Don't let a lot of paint build up. Remember that you want it to look real. Your shading should come in about ¾" from the edges, blending in nicely with the body of the vase as you get further from the edge. Bring the shading inward about 1" from the edges on the shaped base of the vase as well as on the neck to make the object appear to be rounded. The unshaded center area is the highlight that will create the volume as it contrasts with the shaded sides. Smooth out the transition with the paper towel. Remove the stencil.

Tip: Use blue painter's tape under the registration holes so you can find them easily.

2 Position overlay 2 by lining up the holes with the marks from overlay 1. Apply an opaque coat of Antique White to all openings except the bottom base detail. Remember to use a hair dryer to speed things up. Start your shading at the top of the design and follow the instructions within the stencil package. You will apply the Charcoal Grey paint cream along the bottom edges of the top oval and the decorative rings. Apply the Charcoal Grey paint cream to the acanthus leaves where indicated in the instructions to simulate shadow. The bottom base is shaded all over with additional depth at the back edge. Remove the stencil.

3 Overlays 3 and 4 put on the remaining details and use both the acrylic and cream paints. It is amazing to see the progress as you complete each overlay; and when you remove the final one, the result is fabulous!

4 Finishing touches are done without the stencils and are really easy. Use Charcoal Grey to shadow along the underside of each of the light-colored diagonal ribs. You can also add more shadow to the left side. After we add some vines to the wall, we will finish the project by adding cast shadows to everything.

Project 11:
Cottage Creeper

Materials:

Stencil
Cottage Creeper

Paints
Black Forest Green acrylic
Charcoal Grey paint cream
Forest Green acrylic
Mint Julep Green acrylic
Payne's Grey acrylic
Russet acrylic

Stencil Brushes
⅛" brush
¼" brushes (2)
1" brushes (3)

Plants are some of the easiest trompe l'oeil images to stencil. They are everywhere and stenciling a vine on your wall is not out of the scope of reality. In fact vines are the easiest things to turn into trompe l'oeil. This free-form vine looks so real you might think you need to water it! I actually used a portion of early growth Harvard Ivy as the model for this design. The ivy grows all over the bricks of my home studio, and makes a tunnel out of my garage door!

In an earlier project, you learned to build a random vine, using an ivy stencil. Although the ivy is lovely, it isn't a true trompe l'oeil design because it has bridges in the stencil that separate the openings. This Cottage Creeper vine is a true trompe l'oeil design and you will learn to create a drop shadow below the vine to make it look so realistic you will be tempted to water it!

To create a random-looking vine, you will be using the stencil both from the right side and from the reverse side. This changes the look of the print. You can also customize it further by just using a part of the design, taping off what you don't want to use. With this goal in mind, you need to pay close attention to which side of the Mylar you are currently using so that all the overlays will line up the same way. When you take your stencil out of the package, use your permanent marker to write a word, any word . . . maybe "Diva" . . . on all three overlays in the same place on the Mylar. Make it big so you can see it. This will help you immediately recognize which side of the stencil you are using.

Stenciling

1 This design works very well growing down the wall at a slight angle. Position overlay 1 on the wall with the leaf tips pointing downward. Tape it in place and mark through the registration holes with a pencil.

2 Load a 1" brush with Forest Green and unload it on the paper towels. Stipple through the leaf openings and cover all evenly.

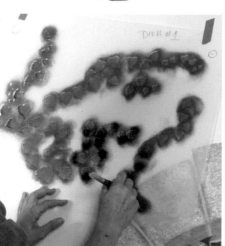

3 Correctly load the ¼" brush with Payne's Grey and add a swirl of shading to the tips of the leaves.

4 Remove the stencil and replace it with overlay 2, stenciling the leaves in the same way, using Black Forest Green and Payne's Grey.

5 Position overlay 3, lining up the holes with the marks. This overlay has both leaf veins and vines.

Start by stenciling the vines, they show up easier because the wall color is visible through the openings. Use the last 1" brush and stencil with Russet. Because the openings are so small, you can get away with using a swirling motion with the brush. Just be sure that you don't have too much paint on it.

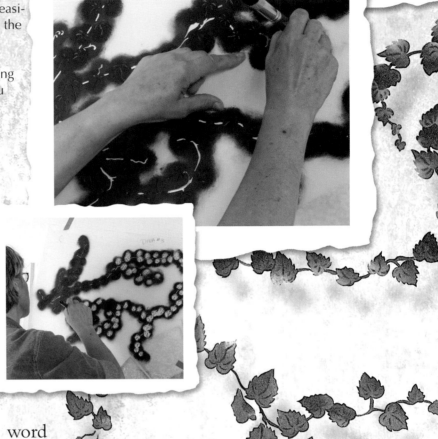

Finish up by using Mint Julep for the leaf veins. It seems to show up better than the Payne's Grey, but you can use that if you wish

To add to the vine, adjust the stencil so that it is going at a little different angle, you can flip it over to the reverse side and stencil it in the same way. Just be sure that the word you wrote on the Mylar reads the same direction when you put up your next overlay. The vine will really look funny if you have one overlay right side up and the others reverse side up. So just pay attention to what you are doing. If you want to use just a part of the vine you can tape off what you don't want to use. Be sure you do this on all overlays . . . I speak from experience!

119

Cast Shadows

The most intimidating aspect of trompe l'oeil for many people is painting a cast shadow. Don't be afraid of this, it is really very easy to do, and the results are phenomenal. It is done freehand . . . No! Don't slam the book closed! This is more like using color crayons than painting . . . it's okay . . . easy now . . . all right . . . calm down. Diva will hold your hand and show you how easy this really is.

Establish a Light Source

We will start with the basics. When light, usually the sun, shines down upon an object, a shadow is cast below and to the opposite side of the light source. It is easiest to use the source of natural light within your room, so if you have a large window use that as your light source. If you don't, don't worry about it. Just pick a logical light source and stick with it as the source of all light within your setting. To make it really simple, if the light is coming from the left, then your shadow will be below and to the right of the object you are shadowing.

This is the most important thing to remember: Keep your light source consistent. The only mistake you can make here is to mix up light sources within the composed setting. And . . .

DON'T RING THE OBJECT WITH SHADOWS.

That simply doesn't work.

We have three projects that need shadowing to make them look real:

In project 8, we shadowed the interior of the niche as part of the stenciling process. Now, after the interior paint has cured, you will go back and add the shadows that create the depth of the niche.

In project 9, you stenciled a vase inside the niche. We will need to add a cast shadow of the vase against the back wall of the niche.

And finally in project 10, you put a vine on the wall that needs a close shadow to make it look like it is actually growing on the wall.

These projects vary in complexity, and to make it easy on you, I am going to handle them in that order starting with the easiest one first, the vine.

Shadowing a Vine

You can create a lot of dimension by the location of the shadows in relation to the position of the vine. There is a great deal of freedom with this process, mainly because any cast-shadowing will make it look dimensional. Just be sure you stick to your light source. Once you get the hang of this it becomes second nature.

If you want it to be growing right tight against the surface, then your shadow will be very close to the vine and leaves.

1 So, here we go . . . take a deep cleansing breath and open that little pot of Charcoal Grey paint cream. Remove the skin from the top of the paint and use the little teensy ⅛" brush to swirl across the top of the fresh creamy surface. Unload it by swirling it on the paper towel. You don't need a whole lot of this on the brush, because you want just a sheer coloring of it.

Note: If you want to make it look as though it is undulating out away from the wall, then you can drop your shadow down, and totally disassociate it from parts of the vine.

2 Now, I said that this is more like coloring than painting and this is what I mean. Hold the brush like a crayon, and scrub it along the surface, don't stroke it, scrub it back and forth, all along the vine, and under the leaves. For the leaves, use a circling motion. To get the shadow right up to the edge of the leaf, go right onto the acrylic; it doesn't effect it in any way. Start lightly, you can always go back and darken it up. Do the entire vine, keeping the shadow consistently below and to one side of the vine. Don't panic if it gets mixed up occasionally, the stencil police will not come and arrest you.

Tip: Remember: "There is no perfect beauty that hath no flaw!" (That's what my boyfriend tells me, isn't that sweet?) This is feeling a bit friendlier now isn't it? The beauty of this stuff is that you can remove it if you goof. All you need is a bit of mineral spirits on a paper towel and wipe it over the area

Casting Shadows of Geometric Objects

Vines were easy. Now we get a bit more technical. Geometrical shapes have rather strict rules regarding shadows. We'll cover the basics first.

Shadows on a Flat Plane

Let us imagine that our vase is standing in the middle of a flat parking lot and the sun is shining upon it from its rightful domain in the sky. The shadow that is cast will be stretched along the ground, in direct relation to the angle of the sun and the height of the vase. You could figure it out mathematically . . . (Oh no, the "M" word again!). But it really isn't that crucial. The shadow would be relatively easy to paint though, because it just goes flat out there.

What if that vase was 6" away from a building, and the angle of the sun was low enough so that the building got in the way of the shadow? What would the shadow do? It would travel along the ground until it came to the building , then it would appear vertically on the face of the building. This is exactly what will happen in the niche.

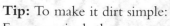

Note: If your shadow appears right next to the object, it will look like it is a flat non-dimensional object.

Tip: To make it dirt simple:
For every inch that you travel horizontally till you hit the "wall," shorten your shadow vertically by the same amount.

Shadowing the Vase

1 I have decided that the light is coming from the right, so the shadow will be cast behind the vase and onto the wall to the left of it. Keeping the light source consistent with the shadows in the niche, I started at the front-left corner of the vase and using Charcoal Grey paint cream, scrubbed in a shadow line that goes across the floor of the niche at about a 45° angle until it meets the back wall of the niche.

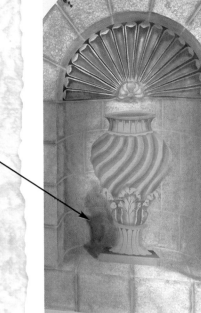

2 Now I start going up the wall, mimicking the shape of the vase at about 6" up from where I am drawing. If you get really confused about this, think of it as though you are bending the vase to make part of it go across the floor and the remaining part go up the wall. That is the shape you will want.

3 Use some mineral spirits on a paper towel to soften the shadow and blend it so that it is even and consistent.

Shadowing the Inner Niche

Adeeper shadow should be applied to the niche, but you will need to wait for a day or two in order for the first shading of paint cream to cure. We are going to use the paper towel as the applicator. This works really well to diffuse the shadow and avoid the streakiness that can occur when you apply it with a brush.

1 Take a paper towel and put a bit of mineral spirits on it. Use the paper towel as an applicator, and twist it into the pot of Ebony Black paint cream.

2 Start at in the right corner of the inner arch and create a line across the niche floor, traveling from the corner to the back edge of the niche near the bottom of the vase.

3 From that point, travel up the back wall of the niche. When you reach the fluting, start arching the line as shown to connect at the top of the niche near the center stone of the window. Why is that? Because the light is hitting the arch and carrying that shape onto the back of the niche. Fill in the area and soften it with the paper towel and mineral spirits.

When you are done, the results will ellicit gasps of awe from friends and relatives. They will ask for the name and number of the professional who did this beautiful thing. You will stand up tall, throw back your shoulders, brush the hair from your eyes causally and say, "Why, I did it myself!"

Yes a diva has been born. Go out and get yourself a tiara, some diva gloves and a work-belt. You've earned it!

125

More Tips from the Diva

- Remember when applying your colors, always start with the lightest color and work to the darkest. You will be much happier with the results. The reasoning behind this is that it is harder to cover up a dark color with a lighter one, and the effect becomes muddy.

- Store your paints in a plastic tub that is easy to carry around. I organize mine by color when I am on a job. That way I know where to find things.

- Always use a separate brush for each color you are stenciling with. You cannot combine colors on one brush because it all becomes the same color after a while. You also cannot wash out a brush and use it right away. This would cause water to run down from the ferrule and dilute your paint, causing run-unders. It may seem rather extravagant, but brushes are your tools, and you need to have enough of them to do the job.

- Large brushes make your job go faster, and their use results in a better looking print. A brush that is too small will give you a polka-dot effect when attempting to cover a large area. The bigger the brush the better coverage you will get.

- If you do get spotty coverage, reload your brush and unload it properly. Then go back over the area, working to fill in the lighter spots and obtain an even coverage. It may take a while, but it will work.

- To help your freshly washed brushes dry faster, place them on a cookie cooling rack and place it by the heat register in the winter and out on the deck or patio in the summer. They dry very quickly that way. One stenciler I know places them in a pillowcase in the dryer . . . I would think it may be a bit noisy, but she swears by it.

- Paint the stencil on paper first. It takes a bit of time, but saves you a lot in the long run. Your stencil will be color coded after that first print and when you get up on the ladder, the job will go much faster for it.

- Don't be afraid if you make mistakes. Remember it's only paint and can be fixed. If it is serious enough, just apply a few coats of the base color right on the area, dry it with a hair dryer and you're ready to go.

- Correcting little mistakes can be done easily with a cotton swab and all-purpose cleaner for acrylic paint and mineral spirits for the oil-based paints.

- If you need to work high on the wall and don't want to rent scaffolding, rig up a portable work surface that will hang around your neck and fasten around your waist. Much like the vendors at the baseball games. Attach little side boxes to it to hold your paints and brushes. You won't be able to reach your carpenter's belt with the box on. Most of all, be careful up there!

- Keep your eyes peeled for anything that may make your stenciling easier. They have many new products coming out, like laser levels that are very affordable and can save you tons of time. Plus, your hubby or significant other will think you're really something if you've got all the latest tools. Just put your name on it and keep it safely tucked away. My tools have a way of disappearing.

- Have fun, accept praise for your efforts, be good to yourself, and be fearless. Good things will come to you, just stay open to all possibilities. Share the love and pay it forward, the world is a better place because you are here.

- Be a Diva!

Checkerboard Allover Repeat Pattern

(for Project 7 on page 100.)

Materials

Clear plastic grid ruler
Craft knife
Metal ruler
Mylar or laminating film
Pencil
Permanent marker with extra-fine tip
Piece of glass

1 Enlarge the pattern below to create your own checkerboard repeat. The squares can be any size. I have found that 3" squares work very well for a large room. You can use graph paper or a hand-drawn 1"-square grid.

Note: I find it easiest to usea clear grid ruler to draw my lines. You can find them at the office superstores. They are really handy because you can see through them to keep your grid lines perfectly equal.

2 Transfer the pattern onto Mylar or laminating film. Just lay it on top and trace it, using the ruler to be certain your lines are straight. Trace the dashed lines to aid you in positioning.

3 Lay the Mylar on a piece of glass and, using the metal ruler to guide the craft knife, cut out the squares. You're ready to go!

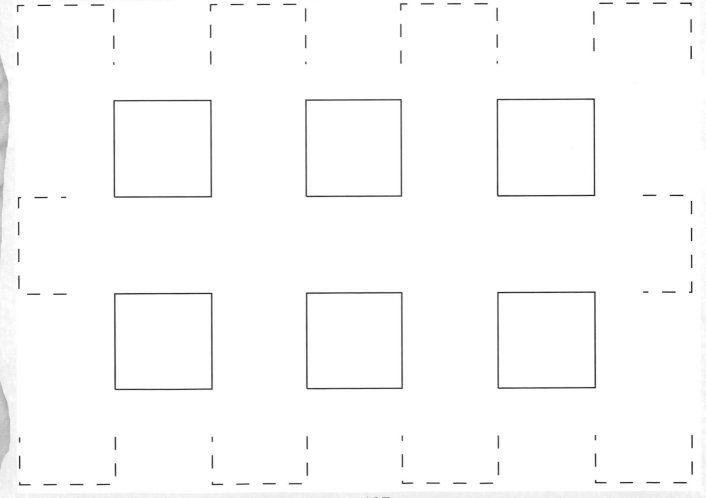

Acknowledgments & Index

- Many thanks and undying gratitude to Jo Packham and Cindy Stoeckl at Chapelle, Ltd., for their patience and faith in me, and for giving me the opportunity to empower mere mortals to unleash the diva within.

- To Brian Morris of Morningstar Photography for capturing it all.

- To my staff at Dressler Stencil Company, Inc., for their patience during the creative process.

- To Paul, the love of my life for being who he is and making sure that I am well taken care of.

- To all the stencil divas everywhere.

If you'd like more information about the products and techniques in this book, visit our website, www.dresslerstencils.com